MHANJ-OCEAN

To the Young
FILMMAKER

To the Young
FILMMAKER

Conversations With Working Filmmakers

RICHARD WORMSER

CENTRAL REGIONAL HIGH SCHOOL
Media Center
Forest Hills Parkway
Bayville, NJ 08721

FRANKLIN WATTS
A Division of Scholastic Inc.

New York • Toronto • London • Auckland • Sydney
Mexico City • New Delhi • Hong Kong
Danbury, Connecticut

Photographs © 2002: Corbis Images: 93, 95 (Bettmann), 59 (Frederick Brown/Reuters NewMedia Inc.), 99 (Vince Bucci/AFP), 82 (Henry Diltz), 11 (Neal Preston), 35 (Rose Prouser/Reuters NewMedia Inc.), 61 (Roger Ressmeyer), 10 (Adam Woolfitt); Globe Photos: 73; Photofest: 24 (Fox Searchlight), 63 (Lifetime Television), 41 (New Line Cinema), 18 (Sony Pictures Classic), 75; Richard Wormser: 85 (Jeremy Francis), 89 (Suzanne Hanover/Monarchy Enterprises BV/Regency Entertainment USA), 13, 16, 27, 33, 38, 45, 66, 68, 79; Robin Holland: 77; W.C. Jersey: 55 (Nick Allen), 49 (Quest Productions), 52.

Library of Congress Cataloging-in-Publication Data

Wormser, Richard, 1933-
    To the young filmmaker : conversations with working filmmakers / Richard Wormser.
        p. cm.
    Includes bibliographical references and index.
    Summary: Profiles of individuals involved in the movie industry—a writer, producers, directors, an actress, and others—offer insights into the process of filmmaking.
    ISBN 0-531-11727-8
    1. Motion pictures—Vocational guidance—Juvenile literature. 2. Motion pictures—United States—Interviews—Juvenile literature. [1. Motion pictures—Production and direction. 2. Motion picture industry.] I. Title
PN1995.9.P75 W67 2002
791.43'023'73—dc21   2001024897

© 2002 by Franklin Watts
All rights reserved. Published simultaneously in Canada
Printed in the United States of America

1 2 3 4 5 6 7 8 9 10 R 11 10 09 08 07 06 05 04 03 02

Contents

Preface 7

INTRODUCTION

The Magic Moments
of Moviemaking 9

CHAPTER ONE

Christine Vachon:
Producing Independent Films 15

CHAPTER TWO

Walter Bernstein:
The Writer's Game 26

CHAPTER THREE

Habib Zargarpour:
The Other Worlds of Visual Effects 37

CHAPTER FOUR

Bill Jersey:
A Documentary Storyteller 48

CHAPTER FIVE

**Lee Grant:
A Woman for All Seasons** *58*

CHAPTER SIX

**Sam Pollard:
Editing—The Heart of the Matter** *65*

CHAPTER SEVEN

**Stephanie Black: Creating
Documentaries and Music Videos** *76*

CHAPTER EIGHT

**Norman Jewison:
A Hollywood Director Follows
His Dream** *87*

Glossary *101*

Additional Information *105*

Index *108*

Preface

When I graduated with a sociology degree from Bucknell University in 1955, I didn't know what kind of job I wanted. I took off for two years, first hitchhiking around America and then spending time in Paris, where I hung out with Allen Ginsberg, Bill Burroughs, and other Beat Generation writers.

Then I got a job as a newspaper reporter in the small town of Shamokin, Pennsylvania. I made my first documentary film in 1963. It was based on an article I had written about mentally disabled children in a state institution. Since then, I have produced, written, or directed more than 100 films.

For this book, I drew on my experiences as a documentary filmmaker. I personally interviewed each filmmaker featured in this volume. I selected these eight working filmmakers based on the quality of their work and the diversity of their experience. They are writers, producers, directors, actors, visual-effects specialists, and editors. They have worked on Hollywood, independent, and television feature films as well as documentaries, cable-television programs, and music videos. I hope their stories encourage young readers to find out more about careers in filmmaking.

Most professionals recommend studying filmmaking in college or at a film school. Some film students work as unpaid interns for a production company or a television network to learn the business firsthand and to make contacts. Most people who get to the top of the ladder begin at the bottom.

Certainly, breaking into the Hollywood or television world is a challenge. These days, however, with low-cost, high-quality digital-video camera equipment and computer-editing programs, most people can make and edit their own films. All you need is a camera, some film, lights, friends, a little money—and a dream.

The most rewarding part of my career has been the privileged access I was given into people's lives. They showed me their pain and their dreams so that I might tell their stories honestly. This experience has enriched my life and, I hope, has touched the hearts of my audience.

—Richard Wormser

Introduction

The Magic Moments of Moviemaking

"Quiet on the set!" shouts the assistant director. All conversation stops and all movement freezes. Everyone remains completely still at this magic moment. The director leans forward and the camera begins to roll at twenty-four frames per second. That is the speed needed to project motion-picture images onto a screen so that the action looks and sounds natural. "Action!" calls the director. The actors begin to speak their lines and the movie comes to life.

This is a standard scene in the making of a feature film—a film that tells a story using actors. The story is the heart of filmmaking. Movies are a modern way of telling stories. Some amuse and delight us. Some entertain and teach us.

All films—from the smallest to the most elaborate—are organized in four stages: development, preproduction, production, and postproduction. The development stage is the planning stage. At this point, the material is chosen or assigned, a budget is prepared, some casting of the actors is done, and the money to go into preproduction is acquired.

The preproduction phase of a feature film includes writing the script, hiring staff and crew, choosing the locations, and casting and rehearsing the actors. Any special computer-generated

Film rolls on the set of a Western movie. For this film, production has begun!

effects are planned, sets are designed and built, and equipment is rented.

Production is the film's shooting stage. Mobilizing a crew for a shoot is a bit like mobilizing an army for battle. Think of the producer as the commander in chief and the director as the general. The director has the awesome responsibility of creating the film. Once filming begins, the director rules and, ideally, has complete creative control. This means that the director will select the camera angles for each scene and direct the actors on how to play that scene.

Preproduction includes rehearsing the actors. Here, actors Kim Wayans, David Alan Grier, and Jim Carrey attend a script rehearsal with the crew of the TV program In Living Color *in 1991.*

The producer and the director need many skilled people to help them produce their film. The director works closely with the director of photography, called the DP. The DP creates the lighting for each scene and helps the director select camera angles. The DP usually leaves the actual filming to a camera operator, who is an expert in both the technical and creative aspects of shooting with film and videotape. An experienced sound person is also essential.

The assistant director and the production manager have two of the most crucial jobs on a feature film. The assistant director, or AD, organizes the shooting schedule and coordinates cast and crew. The production manager oversees the daily shooting schedule, the budget, and organizational details of the film.

A production assistant known as a gofer is at the bottom of the pecking order. The gofer is the worker on the set who "goes for" props, equipment, coffee, or whatever else is needed on a moment's notice.

Other important personnel include the art director, who designs the set; the set decorator, who arranges the props; and the property manager, who is responsible for the props for each scene. Costume designers, wardrobe personnel to care for the costumes, makeup artists, and hairdressers are also required. Then there is the script supervisor. This person checks the accuracy of the dialogue and records the type of shot and the lenses used as well as the positions of all physical elements, including the actors' bodies, for matching purposes during editing.

On the film crew are the gaffer, who sets up and operates the lights; the gaffer's chief assistant, or best boy; and the grips, who move equipment and lay down track so that the camera can move smoothly. A film may also have special-effects artists.

When shooting is completed, the film enters the postproduction stage. This stage includes the editing of film and sound, integration any computer-generated effects with the live-action sequences, addition of music, production of the fine cut, and delivery of the answer print. That's the final edited version that the audience sees.

The basic principles of feature filmmaking apply to other forms of filmmaking—from music videos and television situation comedies to TV commercials and student films. Of course, the scale of the production, the type and quality of the equipment, the size of the crew, and the final product varies greatly.

At one time, filmmaking was expensive and few people could afford to make films. These days, young people everywhere are developing the skills of filmmaking at school and at

Special effects can play a large part in the production process. This crew creates fog for an execution scene from the author's TV series called The Rise and Fall of Jim Crow.

home. New digital technologies have made it possible to make low-budget films of good technical quality.

With these opportunities and fertile imaginations, a few University of Central Florida graduates made a relatively inexpensive horror film in 1999 that caught the attention of the world. Called *The Blair Witch Project,* the film grossed more than $125 million! It doesn't happen every day, but it does happen. If you have an interesting story, some equipment, and a few skills, why couldn't you make it happen?

Chapter One

Christine Vachon: Producing Independent Films

When Christine Vachon, producer of some of the most exciting independent features of the last decade, was once asked exactly what a producer does, she replied:

> The job of producer is one of the great mysteries of the moviemaking process. When I'm asked what producers do, I say "What don't they do?" I develop scripts. I raise money. I put together budgets. I negotiate with stars. I match directors with cinematographers, cinematographers with production designers, production designers with location managers. I make sure the shoot is on schedule, within budget, and on track. I hold hands. I stroke egos. I once had to bail an actor out of jail.

Like many people in the film business, Vachon was a movie buff as a child. When she was seven years old, her parents took her to see *Patton* (1970), a film about George S. Patton, the famous World War II general. "In New York, where I grew up, there are what are called art house theaters that showed the great classic films such as *The Rules of the Game* and *The 400 Blows*. If you loved a movie, and wanted to watch a scene again,

CHRISTINE VACHON

Profession: Film producer
Year; place of birth: 1962; New York, New York
Education: B.A., Brown University
Mailing address: c/o Killer Films, 380 Lafayette Street, New York, NY 10012
Career accomplishments: Produced the highly acclaimed *Boys Don't Cry* (1999)
Selected films (as producer unless noted): *Hedwig and the Angry Inch* (2000), *Velvet Goldmine* (1998), *Happiness* (1998), *Kids* (1995), *Safe* (1995), *Go Fish* (1994, executive producer), and *Poison* (1991)
Words of wisdom: "What I truly believe is that if you fashion a great work, it will ultimately be seen. I have to believe that or I wouldn't be doing what I'm doing."

---

you had to go back and sit through the whole thing again. I sat through *The Poseidon Adventure* five times," she says.

Vachon attended college at Brown University in Providence, Rhode Island, and she studied film theory in France at the University of Paris. At the same time, she deepened her understanding of the media by watching the work of top French and European filmmakers. "My underlying conviction is that the more you know about the history of film, the better you can imagine its possibilities," explains Vachon.

Christine Vachon began working in films in New York in the 1980s. She worked as a gofer on independent films. Because gofers are not well paid, Vachon also worked at night as a freelance copy editor for law firms. Vachon says:

> I had lots of jobs: assistant editor, location scout on music videos, second-unit coordinator, second assistant director. One of the jobs in which I learned the most was script supervisor. My job was to make sure that the scene is getting all the coverage it needs and that there is continu-

ity from one scene to the next. This job taught me how low-budget films get covered—that is, how you can shoot a scene with a minimum number of takes and angles.

In 1987, Vachon and two college friends founded a non-profit production company to make independent films. One of those friends was creative filmmaker Todd Haynes. Vachon explains her dream:

> From the beginning, I always wanted to make films that were both avant-garde and entertaining. While it is true that in the best of all possible worlds, independent films are genuinely alternative, genuinely original versions . . . there's still an economy at work.

Vachon and Haynes shared the same vision. Their films explored serious subjects in an imaginative way. The characters often had sexually and morally unconventional lives. Christine Vachon produced a number of "risky" short films financed by grants and an independent investor. Small theaters showed their films.

By 1991, Vachon had raised enough money to produce her first feature. The project was financed by members of Todd Haynes's family, along with some foundations and agencies, including the National Endowment for the Arts (NEA). This modest but edgy film, called *Poison*, featured three intercut stories, one of which dealt with a homosexual relationship in prison.

When word got out that government funding had gone to a "homoerotic film," there was an uproar in Congress. Newspapers across the country carried the story, as did the television show *Entertainment Tonight*. Vachon regretted that the scandal almost destroyed the NEA, but it helped establish her film company. "The bottom line was a $50,000 opening weekend at the Angelika Film Center in New York—a record that wasn't broken for years," she says. *Poison* also won the 1991 Sundance Festival's Grand Jury Prize.

From that point on, Vachon produced a number of films that received good critical reviews while making a modest profit. They included *Swoon*, *I Shot Andy Warhol*, and one of her favorite films, *Safe*, starring Julianne Moore, who later starred in *Hannibal*. *Safe* told the story of a rich married woman in Los Angeles who wakes up one day to realize that modern society—with its mass production of chemical toxins—is poisoning her. "The film got very little distribution when it was released in 1994," Vachon notes sadly. "Only now is it being recognized as one of the masterpieces of the 1990s."

Christine Vachon produced Safe, *starring Julianne Moore, shown here in a still from the 1995 film.*

Development: Getting a Film Off the Ground

Making a film costs money—usually lots of money—and the producer's job is to find investors. For most dramatic films, producing begins with an idea. Film ideas can come from many sources—from an original idea, a book, a play, a newspaper or magazine article, a historic event, or an old movie. Once a producer has the rights to an exciting idea, a writer has to develop a story treatment—a detailed outline of the film.

The next step is to package it. Those who put up money for a film—whether it is a major studio or a group of independent investors—expect the producer to line up some major talent to make the film. For many Hollywood productions, this usually means having at least one big-name star plus a top writer and director who are committed to, or strongly interested in, the project. A Hollywood producer named Art Linson, who persuaded Robert De Niro to agree to play Al Capone in *The Untouchables* and Brian De Palma to direct the film, got an almost $25-million budget from the studio.

Vachon's budgets are much more modest, and until recently, she did not work with big-name actors. Her selling point is the quality of the actors, the director, and the script.

The cost of a movie is broken down in a budget. Budgets are divided into two main categories, above-the-line and below-the-line costs. Above-the-line costs usually include the cost of talent—producers, writers, actors, and directors. Below-the-line costs include the cost of the crew, staff, equipment, office rental, legal and accounting fees, and location. Postproduction items range from paper clips, insurance, and photocopies to laundry. The above-the-line costs are usually fixed. The below-the-line costs often vary. Most producers ask for more money than they need because they know that backers will generally offer them less than they ask for.

Producers often say that only 15 percent of the budget should pay for the producer, the script, and the director: 5 percent for the producers' category; 5 percent for the writer and script category; and 5 percent for the director's category. This way, 85 percent is "on the screen," where it can be seen.

Producers may seek money for their films from Hollywood studios, television or cable networks, advance foreign sales, home-video companies, or independent investors. Some Hollywood companies are willing to spend hundreds of millions of dollars on a picture while others spend only a few million or less. A truly desperate producer may use personal credit cards, grants, a second mortgage, or money from friends and family.

Because Vachon's movies are quality films dealing with complex subjects, rather than blockbuster action films loaded with stars, she must convince potential investors that her films have a market. She knows most people invest money to make money—not to support the arts. She explains:

> The movies have to go to the marketplace and people have to want to see the movies. Much of the money I get comes from Hollywood sources, and not because they want to underwrite my brilliant career. To do what I do I have to believe the films are so vital that they will find an audience—or at least create one of their own.

Green Means Go!

The sweetest words a producer can hear are "green light." That means a funder has approved the financing, and preproduction can begin. The producer hires the required staff and crew and makes sure that everyone and everything is prepared.

The script is broken down scene by scene and shot by shot. Every item must be included—from the locations being used to the clothing of the actors, the furniture, the lighting, the props, and hundreds of other details. The breakdown also outlines how long it will take to do each scene, how many people and what equipment will be needed, what locations will be used, what sets must be built, and how everybody will be moved to and from every location.

Part of Christine Vachon's strategy as a producer is to prepare every last detail carefully before shooting begins. She also has back-up plans in case things go wrong. Vachon explains:

> When you start each day, you want to know where your lights will be placed, where your camera will be, where you'll store the equipment, where your actors will dress and be made up, and so on. To do this means people have to go to every location in advance and plan these things and see what potential problems may exist. Sometimes, the unexpected happens. You're shooting a scene in a shower and suddenly a water pipe bursts. Or construction starts on the street the very day you plan to shoot. The more you can anticipate these things, the fewer problems you'll have when shooting starts.

Once the camera starts to roll, the producer concentrates on crisis management to ensure that the production is on schedule and within budget. "Until you go into production," Vachon notes, "a budget is an educated guess of what things should cost." Once in production however, budgets must be as close to reality as possible. While Vachon says that low-budget movies are often "a crisis waiting to happen because you have very little slack if something goes wrong," economic disasters can happen to a big-budget movie too.

Waterworld, a 1995 film produced by and starring Kevin Costner, deals with a future time when the world is flooded and what is left of the human race lives on boats in the ocean. The film went $50 million over budget and sank beneath the waves financially. In 1997, *Titanic* also went way over its $100-million budget and yet made more than $1 billion.

Producer's Nightmares

The expression "If anything can go wrong, it usually will" seems to ring true for all productions. The producer's job is to prevent problems and minimize the damage when problems do crop up. Christine Vachon says:

> When a crisis occurs, I feel that one of my greatest responsibilities is to set a tone of calm no matter what the problems. Sometimes I have to fake confidence a lot. I also

have to fake calm. I cannot let the crew see that I have doubts or anxieties even though I may have doubts and anxieties. When people come to me with their problems, needing more time for this, not having the proper equipment for that, I have to assure them that no matter what the problem is, somehow we'll solve it.

Perhaps the worst nightmare for a producer is to lose part of the film's financing at the last minute. This happened to Christine Vachon in a film about the rock music scene of the 1970s called *Velvet Goldmine*. It was budgeted for $4 million, but just as production was about to begin, the backer pulled out.

Vachon had to ask department heads to cut their budgets and salaries. She had to drop scenes and expensive sets and find cheaper locations. "It was the most difficult—and exhilarating—shoot I've ever worked on," Christine Vachon says. She explains:

> I have to make sure not to let the problems affect the director. At the same time, I have to protect the integrity of the film, especially when changes need to be made. I have to ensure that the original vision of the film is not buried underneath the mechanics of filmmaking.
>
> A movie is a very fragile thing, a thing that requires imaginative leaps and an incredible emotional commitment. But no matter how deep and poetic and delicate an on-screen moment will be, you still need lights, camera crew, actors, and a location.

Cutting scenes to save time and money can be a challenge. Vachon explains:

> You try and cut out scenes that you feel can be lost without disturbing the flow or the intent of the picture. Or you tell the director that you don't have enough time to do a certain shot the way you wanted to.

> I remember in one film I produced the director was looking forward to doing a scene that would have taken six hours to light, at least an hour to rehearse before shooting began—and we were three days behind schedule. I told him he'd have to figure out a way to do the scene in four hours total. He ranted and raved and screamed that I was thwarting his creativity. I said he could do the scene his way if he would pay for the cost overrun. Needless to say, he found a way to do it in four hours. I was on his hate list, but that comes with the territory.

At the end of each day of shooting, the film is sent to a laboratory for processing. The director and producer usually review the footage the next day. The footage is called "dailies" because it is a day's shooting. Reviewing the dailies allows the producer and director to shoot something over if there are technical problems or poor performances. If the footage is good, it goes to the editing room, where the editor begins to assemble it into scenes. The editing process takes months. Occasionally an editor asks for extra shooting to make a scene work better. Most producers try to budget for this possibility.

Once the editor has edited the film, the titles and graphics are added and the sound mix is completed. Then a final print comes from the lab. Now the film is ready for distribution.

A distributor makes additional prints of the film, designs advertisements, sets up publicity, and arranges for movie theaters to show the film. Many films have distributors right from the beginning. Sometimes the producer has to get a distribution deal after the film is completed. Independent producers such as Vachon may play a major role in marketing the film. The producer may also enter the movie in important film festivals such as Sundance in the United States and Cannes in France.

Worth the Hard Work

Despite the many trials and tribulations of producing, the joys eventually outweigh the aggravations. For Christine Vachon, the joy of filmmaking is keeping independent films alive as a vibrant and important art form.

One of Vachon's most recent triumphs was *Boys Don't Cry*, a film based on the true and tragic story of Teena Brandon, a young woman whose decision to live her life as a young man led to her murder. The project got off to a rocky start. MGM Studios agreed to finance the $2-million budget but pulled out after giving the project the green light. Vachon scrambled to find another backer. She also lacked a lead actor until the last minute when Hilary Swank read for the part.

Hilary Swank is shown here with Chloë Sevigny (left) in a still from Christine Vachon's Boys Don't Cry. *Swank won the Academy Award for best actress in 1999.*

After its release, the film won many awards, including an Academy Award for Swank and an Academy Award nomination for Chloë Sevigny. Christine Vachon was satisfied with the impact the film made on its audiences:

> I think we were able to present to audiences a character about whom they had no idea and lacked the tools to identify with. By the end of the film, they could understand the character's dilemma and that person was no longer foreign to them.

Although Vachon has had critical success and now works with stars such as Robin Williams and Glenn Close, raising money for her projects is still a challenge. However, Christine Vachon remains true to her original vision to produce films that are works of art as well as entertaining.

Chapter Two

Walter Bernstein: The Writer's Game

"My family wanted me to be a doctor," Walter Bernstein remembers with a smile, "but I knew from early on that I was going to be a writer." As a child, Bernstein wrote short stories and was passionate about movies. For him, the movie theater was a house of magic.

In the era before television, movies fueled the imagination of children throughout the world. "On Saturdays, the movie theater to which I went had a special triple feature instead of the normal double feature, plus cartoons, a serial, and a coming attraction," he explains.

As a young teenager, Bernstein had a bar mitzvah—the ceremony that marks the entry into manhood for Jewish boys. Afterwards, Bernstein and his friends slipped off to the movies without telling anyone. When he emerged, he found the police looking for him. His mother was sure he had been kidnapped since he was carrying $175 in gold pieces he had gotten as gifts!

In the mid-1930s, the sixteen-year-old Bernstein traveled to Europe. Adolf Hitler controlled Germany, and fascism was threatening all of Europe. The communists organized the

WALTER BERNSTEIN

Profession: Writer and writing professor
Year; place of birth: 1919; Brooklyn, New York
Education: B.A., Dartmouth College
Mailing address: c/o Da Capo Press, 11 Cambridge Center, Cambridge, MA 02142
Career accomplishments: Wrote and produced *Fail Safe* for television (2000)
Selected films (as writer unless noted): *The House on Carroll Street* (1988, writer and producer), *Little Miss Marker* (1980, writer and director), *The Front* (1976), *The Molly Maguires* (1970), and *Fail-Safe* (1964)
Words of wisdom: "Don't expect instant success. It's often a long, painful process before someone even agrees to read what you've written."

only resistance to the Nazis. Bernstein was deeply impressed with the European communists' sense of solidarity and courage.

When Bernstein returned to the United States, he went to Dartmouth College in Hanover, New Hampshire, where he joined the Young Communist League, read great European and American novelists as well as Karl Marx, and watched Russian movies. "The books opened my head. The movies opened my heart. A new world was being created and I wanted to be part of that creation," Bernstein explains.

Bernstein also wrote for student newspapers and began writing fiction. He sent a story to *The New Yorker*, the top literary magazine. To his delight, the story was accepted. "I received a check for fifty dollars," he recalls. "It enabled me to prove to my parents that I could make a living as a writer."

When Bernstein graduated from college, the world was on the brink of war. The Soviet Union, once the leader of the fight against fascism, had signed a nonaggression pact with

Germany, dismaying communists everywhere. During the 1930s, a reign of terror and famine had spread throughout Russia. Millions of Russians had been executed, starved to death, or imprisoned. Walter Bernstein, unaware of the mass killings, remained sympathetic to the principles of communism.

When America entered World War II in 1941, Bernstein joined the U.S. Army. Because of his writing skills, he was sent overseas as a war correspondent for an army magazine called *Yank*. In 1944, he managed to smuggle himself into Yugoslavia with a band of guerrillas to interview their leader—Marshal Tito.

After a seven-day march through the mountains, dodging the German planes that bombed the area, he finally arrived at Tito's mountain headquarters. Bernstein got the interview but was arrested by the British immediately afterwards for illegally entering the country. The American army, furious at what he had done, threatened to court-martial him. He was not allowed to publish his interview.

Becoming a Scriptwriter and a Communist

Shortly after the war ended, Bernstein was discharged. He decided to do two things—write scripts for the movies and join the Communist Party.

Bernstein became a journalist for *The New Yorker* after the war. After a book he published received good reviews, he was offered a ten-week contract in Hollywood. He says:

> I had gone to Hollywood with hope and remained with pleasure. I loved being inside a studio, watching how a film was made, the craft that went into it, the teamwork among the makers, and the pride they took in their work. I had always thought of Hollywood as a combination dream palace and moneymaking machine. But it was a major industry as well in which technicians and creative people worked together to make movies.

Working with top directors and other writers, Bernstein learned his craft. One of the first things he learned was the "bang-bang school of storytelling." Says Bernstein:

> What counted was not what was happening now but what happened next—and the sooner you got to it, the better. I discovered that there are three main elements in a feature script—character, content, and meaning. You have to answer these questions: Who are your people and what motivates them? What is the dramatic action—that is, the conflict—and what's it all about?

Bernstein feels that the scripts written for the movies in the 1930s and 1940s were more literate and verbal than scripts written today—the dialogue was sharper, the plots were clearer, the characters were better drawn, and the films had more meaning.

"Today's scripts often rely too much on visual effects, sacrificing a coherent story," he says. "Violence is portrayed for its own sake. Not that good films aren't made anymore. They are. But I feel mega-action films and technology dominate the market."

The United States and the Soviet Union were struggling in the Cold War after the end of World War II in 1945. Anti-communist feeling in America was intense. Tens of thousands of Americans who had joined the Communist Party when Russia was a U.S. ally against the Nazis now faced widespread condemnation. "America was not like Europe where you could be a communist without stigma. In America, you could be ostracized or lose your job," explains Bernstein.

Bernstein returned to New York just when congressional investigating committees began to seek out communists in Hollywood. Communists or communist sympathizers were now being blacklisted. "The charge that we wanted to overthrow the government by violence was ridiculous," says Bernstein. "No one I knew in the party ever dreamed of it. I took it for granted that I could be both radical and accepted, since that had always been the case."

Television Work

Bernstein began to write for television. In those days, television dramas were filmed live. He says:

> Television then was new. It was exciting. It was a blank slate. "Is it film?" we asked. "Is it theater?" The fact that it was live brought it closer to theater. On the other hand, you shot it with a camera. Although you rehearsed beforehand with both actors and camera angles, once the show was on the air, you could not stop it. There were no retakes. You could not edit what you shot. You used three cameras and switched between them as you went. An actor who missed a line had to improvise.

Writing for television situation comedies and dramas is different from writing Hollywood films. While it may take years for a film script to make it onto the screen, a television script gets onto the screen almost every week. A television show's format, length, and characters restrict the scope of the writing. In a feature film, the writer is free to write about any subject.

Another difference between writing for television and writing for Hollywood is the connection to the audience. Television can be closer to a play and more intimate than a movie. Situation comedies are still primarily shot on sets, where the emphasis is more on dialogue and character. Today, of course, many dramatic television shows are shot like movies—on real locations with emphasis on the visuals. But no matter what the form, the common thread that links all material written for mass audiences is that the script must tell a compelling story.

The Blacklist Years

In 1950, Bernstein received bad news from his agent. The television networks had blacklisted him. He was unofficially banned from working in movies or television.

In order to write, Bernstein could do one of two things. He could take a false name and try to write under it. Of he could admit he was a communist to a congressional investigating committee, cut all ties with the communists, and provide the names of other members of the party. "If you wanted to write for television or the movies, you had to become an informer," explains Bernstein. "You had to name other people who were in the party. The committee already knew who these people were . . . but they wanted to demonstrate their power over you."

As anticommunism reached a frenzy, self-appointed anticommunist committees gave television stations lists of so-called communist actors, writers, and directors. If the station did not fire them, the committees organized write-in campaigns to the shows' sponsors and urged viewers not to buy the sponsors' products. A wave of fear spread over the industry. Hundreds of men and women were fired from their jobs, because they had been accused of being communists or communist sympathizers—often without evidence.

Walter Bernstein decided to write under a false name. Taking the name Paul Bauman, Bernstein began to write scripts for a TV series called *Danger*. Then the networks began to insist on meeting writers to confirm their identities. Bernstein could no longer hide under a false name and his agent dropped him.

Bernstein was forced to find a "front"—someone who would pretend to be the writer of his scripts. As he searched, Bernstein was painfully aware he had become an outcast in the television community. People he had worked for in the past now crossed to the other side of the street when they saw him. Others told him privately that while they hated the blacklist and didn't care about his political life, they would lose their jobs if they gave him work.

"People were scared—and with good reason," explains Bernstein. "Witch-hunting had extended to anyone helping the witch. And I was considered a witch. Even magazine assignments dried up. Blacklisted people were banished from professions they had spent their lives practicing."

Finally, Bernstein found a woman willing to be a front—for 25 percent of his fee. For a while it worked. But one day she tearfully told Bernstein she had to quit. Her analyst told her that what she was doing was bad for her self-esteem! Occasionally, a writer who was not blacklisted would allow Bernstein to use his name on a script. Eventually, Bernstein and two other blacklisted writers formed a collective and shared whatever work they could get.

Work began to flow in from the CBS television network. The network was producing a new weekly show called *You Are There*. In the series, reporter Walter Cronkite interviewed actors playing historical figures such as Socrates and Joan of Arc. Bernstein and his friends wrote for the show, although they had to use fronts. For the writers, it was a great opportunity to write scripts that expressed their ideals. "We tried to celebrate the human spirit, to show the forces throughout history that had tried to stunt and oppress that spirit, and to explain as clearly as we could its victories and defeats," he says.

The network knew that Bernstein and the others were writing the scripts, but no one complained because the show was a hit. As long as everyone kept quiet, the work kept coming.

After the death of Soviet premier Joseph Stalin in 1953, the Soviet Union began to reveal the enormity of his crimes. "Everything our enemies had said about Stalin proved to be true. I was devastated," Bernstein recalls. When the Soviet Union crushed an uprising against communism in Hungary, Bernstein, along with thousands of other communists, left the Communist Party.

By the 1960s, blacklisted writers, actors, and directors started to work under their own names again. Bernstein was hired for a feature film for Paramount Studios. After eight years, his life seemed about to return to normal when he was called to testify before the House Committee on Un-American Activities. Paramount insisted that he testify before the committee and name names to keep his job.

Bernstein told the studio that if he had to testify before the committee, he would talk about himself, but he would not name names. Paramount surprised Bernstein by telling him to either name names or to not testify at all. Bernstein chose not to testify. Two weeks later, Paramount cleared him. He was finally off the blacklist. "I was working again in movies. I would find a community there. But I still lived in a country where there would be no shortage of injustice and inequality. There was still a better world to be made," Bernstein says.

Writing for Hollywood

To help make that better world, Bernstein and his good friend director Martin Ritt wrote a film script called *The Molly Maguires*. Sean Connery played the lead role. The script was based on the true story of a secret organization of Irish coal miners battling against the mine owners in the anthracite coal region of Pennsylvania. Working and living conditions were horrible, and the Mollies, as they were called, were willing to use violence to achieve their goals. An Irish informer had infiltrated their organization. He eventually testified against them, and nineteen men were hanged. Later, many felt that he had given false evidence.

In 1970, Bernstein wrote a script about his experience during the blacklist period called *The Front*. A major studio liked the idea but wanted a big-name actor like Robert Redford or Warren Beatty to play the lead role. They had no success. Then Martin Ritt, the director, suggested that they make the film a comedy and hire an up-and-coming young actor/director—whose name he couldn't remember. It turned out to be Woody

Walter Bernstein (left) confers with Woody Allen (right) on the set of The Front, *written by Bernstein in 1970.*

Allen! Allen agreed to do it, and Bernstein was nominated for an Academy Award for his script.

Thoughts About Writing

A script usually begins with an outline or treatment. The script itself is a blueprint for the film. It is broken down into scenes and contains a description of the action, dialogue between the actors, and possible camera angles.

Most writers do not have ultimate control of their scripts. Directors or studios modify the scripts of even the best writers. Only in the theater, protected by the Dramatists Guild, do writers have complete control over their scripts. In many television series, a team of writers and producers review scripts. Sometimes actors want to change lines, or even change the nature of their character.

Although most films do not begin shooting until the script is close to its final form, this is not always the case. Bernstein had one assignment for a 1960 film called *Heller in Pink Tights*, starring Sophia Loren. "They already had a script but it needed changes and they were ready to start shooting. So every day I was locked into a hotel room and I wrote the scenes that would be used the next day. They made the whole film that way. It wasn't a bad film actually, but the studio decided that they didn't like the cut and changed it in the editing—for the worse, in my judgment," explains Bernstein.

Scripts may be based on an original idea such as *The Front* or may be adapted from a book. One of Bernstein's most successful scripts was based on the book *Fail-Safe*. It was about a fictitious confrontation during the Cold War between the United States and the Soviet Union in which a rogue American general orders an atomic attack on Russia.

Today, writing scripts is highly competitive. The first task for an unknown writer is to write a good script. Then he or she must find an agent. The agent works as a go-between with the studios or television networks and the writer.

Getting an agent can be difficult, however. Agents are swamped with requests from writers to read their work and represent them. Most agents hire readers to look over scripts. The agent reads only the promising ones. An agent who likes a script will try to arrange a meeting between the writer and producer to pitch—or present for sale—the idea.

Today, Walter Bernstein continues to write features for television. His film *Miss Evers' Boys*, for the HBO cable network, won the Humanitas Prize. He recently wrote the live teleplay remake of his hit 1964 script *Fail-Safe* with actors George Clooney and Noah Wyle for CBS television.

George Clooney (left) and Noah Wyle shown during a press conference to promote their performances in Fail Safe, *a live two-hour television movie written by Walter Bernstein.*

Walter Bernstein also teaches screenwriting at Columbia University. He tells his students:

> Look at as many films as possible, not just films made today but old films as well. It's hard to sell a script to Hollywood. Fortunately, cable television shows a lot of movies. And many filmmakers today are going the independent route, raising their own money and making their own films.
>
> The principles of script writing remain the same: the story line must be clear and well structured, and the characters must be interesting. Also, the story must have meaning, it must say something to people. Ask yourself, "What am I saying and why am I saying it?"
>
> And then you must write. Write every day if you can. Learn your craft. You have to be dedicated, driven to write.

Chapter Three

Habib Zargarpour: The Other Worlds of Visual Effects

An earthquake triggers a volcanic explosion beneath a city. Lava flows like a raging river through city streets, dissolving buildings, cars, and trapped citizens in its path. An ocean liner fills with water, breaks in two, and sinks to the bottom of the ocean, dragging hundreds of passengers and crew with it. Two enemy aerial fleets meet in the farthest region of outer space and fight to the death. A man grabs his chin and pulls his face off, revealing another face underneath it. A raptor and a tyrannosaurus furiously tear into each other until the tyrannosaurus seizes the raptor by the neck, swings it in the air, and hurls it to the ground.

Unlike documentary filmmakers whose in-depth exploration of reality reveals the world as it is, visual-effects specialists use illusion to show us worlds that we cannot see or experience. They blend human imagination with the wonders of technology.

The world of visual effects is almost as old as movies. In 1893, Thomas Edison invented the motion picture in America. His first films showed documentary scenes of daily life: people on the street, a train entering a station, a performer dancing, someone doing gymnastics. Films soon began presenting sto-

HABIB ZARGARPOUR

Profession: Visual-effects specialist

Year; place of birth: 1964; Tehran, Iran

Education: B.A.S.C., University of British Columbia in Vancouver, Canada; graduated from the Art Center College of Design

Mailing address: c/o Industrial Light & Magic, Lucas Digital, P.O. Box 2459, San Rafael, CA 94912

Career accomplishments: Was nominated for Academy Awards for visual effects for *The Perfect Storm* and *Twister*

Selected films: *The Perfect Storm* (2000), *Star Wars: Episode I—The Phantom Menace* (1999), *Star Trek: First Contact* (1996), *Twister* (1996), *Star Trek: Generations* (1994), and *The Mask* (1993)

Words of wisdom: "The computer is only the technical means. Digitalization allows the artist to extend his palette. But, in filmmaking, his creation serves a larger purpose—to enhance the story and the characters. Both are still the keys to a good film."

---

ries as if they were plays. Because film was silent, actors would stand on a stage and read lines from title cards.

In 1895, a director named Alfred Clark invented a new language for movies, then called kinetoscopes. He was directing a film called *The Execution of Mary Stuart*—a reenactment of the execution of Mary, Queen of Scots, in 1587. Clark staged a scene in which the executioner raises an ax over the actor playing the queen, who is resting her head on a chopping block. The filming was then stopped, and the actor was replaced by an identically dressed dummy. Then the filming started again as the executioner brought his ax down on the head of the dummy. Many people were unaware that a dummy had been substituted for the actor and believed an actor was actually beheaded. It was of one of the first special effects.

In 1902, Georges Méliès, a French filmmaker, began to create a world of visual effects in a film he made called *Voyage to the Moon*. Méliès, a professional magician, used a variety of tricks to create some fantastic effects. With a combination of animation, special sets, stop-motion, and makeup, he created a low-tech fantasy world in which scientists on Earth visit the moon. It was the first step on a road that would eventually lead to the amazing visual effects of today's Hollywood films.

When they discovered that one image could be superimposed over another, special-effects artists found a whole new world opening to them. A ghost could be seen rising from a grave, for example. First, the empty grave was shot and then a figure wearing a white shroud was filmed rising up on a neutral background. The two images were then placed on top of each other, creating the illusion that the figure was actually rising from the grave.

In the 1930s, horror films advanced the techniques of special effects even more. Floods, earthquakes, wild animals, monsters, and ghosts became common. Films such as *King Kong*, which blended the animated figure of a giant ape with live actors, thrilled world audiences. Other films, such as *Buck Rogers* in 1939 and *The War of the Worlds* in 1953, created primitive effects of traveling through outer space or battling against alien invasions. Miniature models filmed in close-up, animation, special camera tricks and laboratory processes, and actors wearing elaborate makeup and costumes created many of the effects. They were often obvious and easy to spot. But most audiences were willing to suspend their critical eye and enjoy the effects.

Effects continued to improve and become more sophisticated until a revolution in the 1970s. A young filmmaker by the name of George Lucas came up with an idea that would involve creating a whole world of special effects. His film, *Star Wars*, told of a battle between the forces of good and the forces of evil in outer space.

To carry out his vision, Lucas created a company dedicated to developing visual effects. It was called Industrial Light

& Magic (ILM). Over the next twenty-five years, ILM created worlds in which aliens fought with earthlings, miniature soldiers came to life and declared war on the human race, and dinosaurs roamed the land as they had in prehistoric times.

As revolutionary as the technology in *Star Wars* was, filmmaker George Lucas was not satisfied. "I was frustrated because I couldn't do things I imagined. I was stuck with using rubber puppets or with people dressed in rubber masks. Models had to be a certain size. I felt very limited as to how I could tell my story," he later explained.

A New Generation

At the same time, the world of special effects was attracting many of the best and brightest of a new generation of computer artists. Among them was Habib Zargarpour, who was born in Tehran, Iran, and then lived and studied in Canada and the United States. Zargarpour's dream as a teenager was to become an industrial designer. He was a graphic artist and fine-arts illustrator who wanted to design cars and planes, combining his artistic talent with the new computer technology.

In 1990, after reading an article on how the computer was used to create special effects for a film called *The Abyss*, Zargarpour focused his interest on film and three-dimensional graphics. By chance, he became involved in creating a storyboard for a film on a computer. "By the time the job was finished, I was hooked," he says.

In 1993, Zargarpour joined Industrial Light & Magic and worked as technical director on a number of films including *The Mask*, *Star Trek*, and *Twister*. The latter won him an Academy Award nomination in the United States for his computer design of the tornado.

Shortly afterwards, he attended a meeting at which Lucas was about to unveil his latest project. He finally felt that technology had caught up with his imagination. Computer graphics had become digitized. That is, information about shapes, colors, movements, and speech could be transformed into digital

Habib Zargarpour worked on the highly acclaimed special effects in The Mask, *a 1994 film starring Jim Carrey.*

form on a computer. Then this information could be moved and manipulated in an almost infinite variety of ways. Digital technology allowed for much greater freedom and innovation. Visual-effects specialists discovered how to use the computer to create action and characters that could blend seamlessly into live-action scenes.

The project Lucas unveiled was called *Star Wars: Episode I—The Phantom Menace*. He presented to his special-effects team a visual outline of the story organized in some 3,500 storyboards in which the action was sketched out. Zargarpour explains:

> Usually, when we are asked to do a big film as far as special effects are concerned, we are talking about 250 effects. In a monster movie like *Titanic*, there were almost 500

effects. George [Lucas] wanted us to do somewhere around 2,000 effects. This meant that almost every shot would have some sort of a special effect. It was mind-boggling. In the back of my mind I thought, well, somehow I will accomplish this . . . but I didn't know how.

Zargarpour and the ILM team had to deliver a finished project on schedule and within budget. He says:

> The scope of the film was enormous. We had to create all kinds of scenes—battle scenes in which thousands of droids fight against thousands of aliens and humans, scenes in which underwater monsters attack a submarine and one another, and animals stampede through a forest knocking down trees. Each frame had to be filled with all sorts of action so that when the main characters are talking or doing something, fighter planes could be zooming overhead or dozens of people might be busy at one task or another behind them. The storyboard gave us the general idea of what was required. We had to figure out how many characters we had to create and what they might look like, how they might sound, how many models and miniatures we would need.

Getting to Work

The project was broken down into three parts with teams assigned to carry out each section. Leading each team was a visual-effects supervisor who combined creative vision with technical expertise. The crew included producers, computer programmers and designers, technical directors, graphic and digital artists, art directors, model makers, stage technicians, animators, editors, sound technicians, and camera operators.

One of the toughest assignments fell to Zargarpour. He and his team had to design one of the most complex and critical scenes in the film—a high-speed automobile race called the Pod Race.

The sequence centered on a wager between the main character of the film, known as Jedi Master Qui-Gon Jinn (played by actor Liam Neeson) and an alien named Watto, who was computer generated. The bet is that ten-year-old Anakin Skywalker (played by Jake Lloyd), who is Watto's slave and an expert race driver, will win the Boonta Classic Pod Race. If Skywalker wins, the Jedi Master will get a needed part to fix his disabled spaceship and the boy will gain his freedom. If he loses, Watto will own the spaceship and Skywalker remains in slavery.

Zargarpour and his crew had five major items to contend with: (1) the interaction between the actors and the computer-generated characters; (2) the computer-generated characters' interaction with one another; (3) the crowds at the stadium; (4) the terrain over which the race takes place; and (5) the race itself.

It is not easy for actors to act with a computer-generated character. "After all, they must do the scene as if the character is really in front of them when of course there is no one there," explains Zargarpour. The actor does the scene in front of a large blue screen. Later, the blue background is filled in with the computer characters and action images to make it seem as if the action is actually taking place.

Creating the computer-generated characters also was a challenge. Zargarpour says:

> In making a computer character, facial animation and muscular movement are essential. We have to design the character so that the skin fits properly over the muscles, and eye and lip movements are normal. We also developed programs that could simulate fabric movement—how a piece of clothing would move as a computer-generated character walked or ran or fought with another character.
>
> What is especially difficult is to create interactions between computer-generated characters when they hug or touch each other. We have to create a realistic feeling of two bodies making contact.

> Sometimes actors serve as the model for the computer character. To create the character of Jar Jar, we filmed [an actor] who has a marvelous sense of motion. We filmed him walking and then transferred the footage into a computer. Then we created Jar Jar using those movements, which allowed us to make him into a character that is as rich and as human and as dignified as any real character in the movie.

Another challenge for Zargarpour and the visual-effects team was to create a mass audience for the race in the stadium. In the film, hundreds of thousands of people are watching the race. He explains:

> For the long shot of the bleacher scene in the stadium Pod Race, 350,000 Q-tips were painted and used. They were mounted in a model stadium and made to sway from side to side by a fan. From a distance, the Q-tips looked like a large crowd of people following the race from side to side.
>
> But for closer shots, George [Lucas] wanted to give the impression of people behaving just as they would at a ball game. This meant we had to create computer characters that would walk up and down steps or wait in line to use the bathroom or get something to eat. One thing that George noticed as we were working on this sequence—he said all the characters seemed to be alone. So we had to show some people walking and talking together.

One of the critical areas that had to be designed was the landscape over which the cars would race. A car had to appear to be traveling 600 miles (980 km) an hour. The terrain was painted by Doug Chiang, one of the artists, and then entered into the computer.

The key event in this sequence was, of course, the race itself. George Lucas wanted the Pod Race to look like a real car race. So the team watched footage of real car races to see how a car rolls over and disintegrates during a crash. "We wanted to show the pods tumbling, tearing apart but not exploding," says Zargarpour. He explains the process:

> We first intended to do this using miniatures—very small models—of a car. We figured out that to get the effect we wanted—to show what would happen to a car when it crashed at 600 miles an hour—that we would have to have the model go at a speed of 100 miles an hour. This meant dropping the model from a speeding car and hoping that the camera would record the crash. Since each model cost about $50,000 to build—and we weren't sure the scene would work—we decided to animate the crashes in the computer.

Habib Zargarpour uses both models and computers to create his special effects.

> I modified a program that allowed us to emulate rigid body simulation—that is, one that would let us calculate physical action in such a way as to be visually accurate. Thus, for example, it could create the effect of metal folding on the car when it impacts an object and begins to break up. What we were doing was putting the laws of physics to work for us in the computer.

As films rely more and more on the use of computer graphics, some people are concerned that all special effects will be computerized. Zargarpour thinks that day is still quite far off. He says:

> There are certain miniatures that we will always need. In *Star Wars,* miniature buildings were used to create Theed, a city of the future. While explosions can be created on the computer, they are still cheaper to do with models. Sometimes as many as five people may work on a model for weeks, though it will last for only a few seconds on screen before it is blown up.

But computer-generated images are increasingly being used. In large battle scenes such as that between Gungans (good guys) and the battle droids (bad guys), only one Gungan and one battle droid were created on the computer. They were multiplied 4,000 times to give the impression of two armies fighting.

Advice for Students

Today's visual-effects specialist must be highly skilled with a good working knowledge of computer graphics and of computer-operating systems like Unix. Almost every artist has at least a college education, if not an advanced degree, usually in some aspect of graphics and computer science.

Zargarpour advises young people to get a background for this field in high school:

If a young person today wants to make a career in computer animation, he or she can now take courses in this in college, an opportunity that did not exist a few years ago. At the high school level, I would recommend a mixture of the sciences and the arts—math and physics definitely—but also photography, painting, drawing and, of course, filmmaking.

But keep in mind that it's not the computer that creates these worlds. It's the imagination of the person using it.

Chapter Four

Bill Jersey: A Documentary Storyteller

It is hard to imagine that one of the founding fathers of modern documentary filmmaking was forbidden as a child to go to movies. Bill Jersey remembers:

> When I was growing up, I wanted to be liked and approved. I also wanted to be like any other kid. And I couldn't be. My fundamentalist upbringing put strict limits on what I could do. No dancing, no singing—and especially no movies. Just church and more church. With an occasional parade and a trip to the beach.

Jersey's father was a devout Christian who believed that the owners of movie theaters were evil people. The only concession he would make for his children was to buy 8-millimeter films of cartoons and show them at home on a small projector.

As a child, Bill Jersey liked to draw. He loved to sketch pictures of baseball players and cartoon figures. "We didn't have books at home. I think the only books my father read were the Bible and hymnbooks. So drawing became my emotional outlet for me," says Jersey. Later, in high school, Jersey found a way to use the visual skills that connected him with a world in

BILL JERSEY

Profession: Documentary filmmaker

Year; place of birth: 1927; Jamaica, New York

Education: B.F.A., Wheaton College; M.F.A., University of Southern California

Mailing address: c/o Quest Productions, 2600 10th Street, Berkeley, CA 94710

Career accomplishments: Has made more than 200 films. Has also been nominated for several Academy Awards and won numerous Emmy Awards for his television documentaries

Selected films (as producer and director unless noted): *What About God?* (2001), *Naked to the Bone* (1999), *Loyalty and Betrayal* (1994), *Maya Angelou: Rainbow in the Clouds* (1992), *Faces of War* (1986), and *A Time for Burning* (1967)

Words of wisdom: "I feel it's important to record these stories on tape. They are part of our heritage and tell us who we are as a people."

---

which he could not fully participate. "I went to dances with my friends. Since I wasn't allowed to dance, I would take my camera to the dance and snap photographs of the kids dancing and then sell the photographs for a dollar. In that way, I could be part of a world that I really wasn't allowed to enjoy," he explains.

Bill Jersey did not finish high school with his class. Instead, he joined the navy before graduation, just as World War II was ending. The navy introduced him to the world of film. He saw his first movie at the age of eighteen on board a ship! It starred June Allyson. "I thought she was the most beautiful woman I had ever seen and I fell in love with her—and with movies," says Jersey. "I forget the name of the picture."

After the navy, Jersey pursued a career in art. Because his upbringing made him wary about secular schools, he attended a Christian institution called Houghton College. There he had the good fortune to have two extraordinary teachers—Willard and Aimée Ortlip. "They were the kind of people everyone wishes they had as parents. They took me under their wing and taught me much about painting," says Jersey. His education in art continued at Wheaton College in Illinois, where another teacher, Carl Steele, also helped him develop his talents as an artist.

When he finished school, Jersey got a job drawing images for commemorative plates for a company that sold them to a very expensive store. He says:

> Of course, I wasn't paid anything for my work. About ten dollars or so while the company made a good profit on them. I didn't complain because I was delighted that I was getting paid for doing art. But the job taught me two valuable lessons in life. The first is to let yourself be exploited, because if you do—and it's the right kind of job—it gives you the chance to learn a lot very quickly. The second rule is: don't let yourself be exploited for very long.

The Beginning of a Career

In the 1950s, Jersey was offered a job as a set designer for a religious film company called Good News Productions. His job was to draw sketches of the physical environment in which the action took place. If a scene took place in a living room, he would design the room and specify its size, where the furniture should be placed, and what props would be needed. Then members of the scenic crew would build Jersey's set or convert an already existing location to look like Jersey's design. Jersey says:

> I didn't know anything about filmmaking or design for film, but the owner liked my artwork. My father didn't object because the film company made Christian films and as long as they were Christian, that was all right with him. The owner of the company taught me a lesson I never forgot. He

taught me to watch movies with the soundtrack off so that my attention would be focused on the visuals and I could discover what the images had to say to me.

The company was small and Jersey found himself doing a little bit of everything. The experience convinced him to become a filmmaker. Documentaries interested him because he enjoyed working with real people.

In 1954, shortly after Jersey married, he moved to California to study filmmaking at the University of Southern California. There he learned both the craft and art of filmmaking in documentary and dramatic films.

Jersey made a short film in school called *The Black Cat*, based on a story by Edgar Allen Poe. It won him a national award from a major magazine as the best student film. "I looked at it not too long ago," he notes. "I thought it was awful."

After school, Jersey looked for work. He was offered a job as a file clerk—an entry-level position at the CBS television network. He was told that many people started that way and worked their way up into a production position, but he turned down the offer. Having gone to the University of Southern California had its benefits. "If you go to a school where the action is, that's where you'll often find the jobs," says Jersey.

Then a producer came to the school and said he needed an art director and sound person for a low-budget feature film he was doing in the Amazon region called *Manhunt in the Jungle*. Jersey explains:

> I hadn't the faintest idea how to do sound. I began to rush around to learn how to do it. Three days before we were to go to Peru, I learned that they expected me to check out the equipment before it was sent down. Fortunately, I got sick and couldn't do it so the studio in Hollywood had to check it out. When we arrived in Brazil, we found that the camera wasn't working properly. The studio technicians had failed to do their job. So they got the blame instead of me.

Bill Jersey (center) working as sound person and art director on Manhunt in the Jungle, *a 1956 film shot in the Amazon region*

Working on the film was a great opportunity for Jersey. "I was not only the art director, I got to do location scouting and sound. Working on this job with a Spanish crew who knew no English, I built a house that was used as a set. This forced me, of necessity, to learn Spanish. But we got the job done," says Jersey.

Another thing the job taught Jersey was that feature filmmaking was not for him. It kept him away from his family too long. "When I came home to my wife and young baby after

119 days in the Amazon, she said, 'You're going to take a job—or else.' "

For a brief time, Jersey worked for the film division of Western Electric, makers of telephones for phone companies. The conformity the job required convinced Jersey that the corporate world was not for him. His desire to make the best possible film often conflicted with the demands of the corporate world. His dilemma was how to escape from his position and find work in film to support his family.

He decided to convince the corporation to hire Willard Van Dyke, who at that time was one of the best filmmakers he knew, to make a film for them. His plan was to work with Van Dyke, show Van Dyke how good he was, and get hired away from General Electric. The strategy worked! Van Dyke hired Jersey and his career was on track.

Becoming a Documentary Filmmaker

Bill Jersey's career took a big leap forward when he was offered a job as a producer/director on a documentary series for the NBC television network called *The DuPont Show of the Week*. The position allowed Jersey the opportunity to make films about the lives and struggles of real people.

He shot and directed three films about people struggling to help better the lives of others—one was a schoolteacher; another, a parole worker who worked with street gangs; and the third, an ex-convict on parole. "I discovered that it gave me a great deal of pleasure to help people tell their own stories while at the same time telling stories that I believed society needed to hear," he says.

By the 1960s, Bill Jersey, now on his own, had become one of the founding fathers of a new style of filmmaking called *cinema verité*, a French term literally meaning "truth movies"—or films that tell present-day stories about real people. A revolution had taken place in the technology of filmmaking. Camera and sound equipment had become portable.

The technological revolution came at the time of a social revolution. The civil rights and antiwar movements had erupted, and filmmakers were in the front lines recording the struggle. Documentary filmmakers were shooting film in the streets of America and on the battlefields of Vietnam.

In 1968, Bill Jersey was nominated for an Academy Award for *A Time for Burning*. It was one of the first documentaries to tell a real life story in dramatic form. At its center was the struggle of Reverend William Youngdahl, a young Lutheran minister who invited twelve black families to visit his all-white church in Omaha, Nebraska. The invitation produced violent reactions and discord among the congregation. The minister eventually resigned in frustration.

A Time for Burning established Jersey as one of the foremost documentary filmmakers in America. He followed it with *The Season's Change*, a powerful look at the antiwar movement, the police, and politicians at the Democratic Party's 1968 national convention in Chicago.

In 1986, Bill Jersey shot *Faces of War* in El Salvador. The film told the personal stories of six Americans working in the region and served as a fast-paced introduction to the crisis in Central America.

Jersey worked on films about a family struggling to raise a mentally disabled child; Lutheran ministers who lost their churches because of their efforts to help unemployed steelworkers; men and women dying in a hospice; and Elizabeth Eckert, a teenager who worked to integrate Central High School in Little Rock, Arkansas.

For Jersey, the opportunity to make such films was a great privilege. He says:

> I have been privileged that people I don't know—people I never met before I filmed them—have allowed me to enter into their lives. People have let me see their deepest sorrows and their real hopes. They have had the courage and trust to let me show their weaknesses and frailties. And sometimes when I wonder if I have pushed too far, they have rewarded me by telling me, "No. We needed to do this. You have helped us by your film."

Bill Jersey with his camera during the making of Faces of War *in El Salvador in 1968*

In 1990, Bill Jersey filmed at the fortress of fundamentalist education in America—Bob Jones University in Greenville, South Carolina. His film was part of a series on religious fundamentalism. Although the school was wary about allowing outsiders to make a documentary about its activities and beliefs, Jersey's fundamentalist background helped him gain access. "I could sing the hymns they sang, quote the same verses from the Bible, and I was allowed to do something no outsider had ever done—film their institution," he explains.

Jersey found the fifty-year-old institution in a time warp:

> It was as if the 1960s hadn't happened, the women's liberation movement hadn't happened, civil rights hadn't happened, and rock and roll and the Vietnam War hadn't happened. As far as Bob Jones University was concerned, it was a world in which right was right and wrong was wrong and everybody knew the difference.

Although he disagreed with many of the school's teachings, Jersey felt his job as a filmmaker was to let the school tell its own story. In the end, some people believed the film exposed the dangers of the religious right. Bob Jones University officials saw it as a fair and accurate portrait of their institution.

Jersey followed his series on fundamentalism with a two-part documentary film about the history of the Mafia in America called *Loyalty and Betrayal*. His film shared how the mob, whose members were once so loyal that they would willingly die in the electric chair before revealing secrets, became an organization filled with informers. He explains the challenge he faced as a documentary filmmaker:

> These guys were killers. But I felt that if I made a film telling only about how they killed, it would not really be an interesting film. . . . I wanted to show the whole human being, not just how many people they killed. And I made some remarkable discoveries as a result of doing this. One man told me how his uncle, who was his boss, ordered him to kill his best friend. And he did it.

Bill Jersey's most recent two films are for television. One is about the conflict presently raging in America about the teaching of evolution and creationism in the schools. The other is a four-part television series about the African-American struggle for freedom during the era of segregation called *The Rise and Fall of Jim Crow*.

Throughout his long career, Bill Jersey has enjoyed his work as a documentary filmmaker. He says:

> It is one of my greatest pleasures to help people tell their own stories. Stories are important because as a people we are also storytellers. As soon as we begin to talk, we ask mommy or daddy to read us a story. So we tell stories because that's the best way of sharing who we are.

Chapter Five
Lee Grant: A Woman for All Seasons

Most filmmakers specialize. Documentary filmmakers make documentaries. Feature filmmakers make features. But Lee Grant is one of the few filmmakers who is as comfortable as a feature director as she is as a documentary filmmaker. She is also unique because her filmmaking career is an extension of her career as one of America's outstanding actors.

As a child, Lee Grant took ballet, violin, and voice lessons. Her mother worshiped the arts. "It was a mission with my mother. She wasn't an ordinary lady. She was of a totally romantic nature. Fortunately, she had remarkable taste. She bathed in what I was doing," explains Grant. By the time she was six, Lee Grant was performing at the Metropolitan Opera's corps de ballet "even though I was klutzy," she admits.

When Grant attended public school, students from a parochial school harassed her for being Jewish. "They threw nails. They yelled 'Jews killed our Lord.' I felt an outsider in certain ways," says Grant.

Discovering the Theater
The turning point in Lee Grant's life came when she was sixteen. She discovered the Neighborhood Playhouse School of

LEE GRANT

Profession: Director and actor

Year; place of birth: 1927; New York, New York

Education: Trained at the Neighborhood Playhouse School of the Theatre

Mailing address: Feury/Grant Entertainment, 441 West End Avenue, New York, NY 10024

Career accomplishments: Won an Academy Award for best feature-length documentary for *Down and Out in America* (1986). Also won an Academy Award for best supporting actress for *Shampoo* (1975)

Selected films (as director unless noted): *Gun Deadlock* (2001), *Confronting the Crisis: Childcare in America* (1999), *Say It! Fight It! Cure It!* (1997), *Seasons of the Heart* (1994), *Nobody's Child* (1986), *The Willmar 8* (1980), and *Tell Me a Riddle* (1980)

Words of wisdom: "The documentaries that I make are not intended to entertain. They are tools for change."

---

the Theatre and its director and great acting teacher, Sanford Meisner. "It had an enormous effect on me to this day. He gave a very groundless girl a real system of work," she explains.

Lee Grant learned her craft from Meisner:

> He demystified scripts. He made theater real and practical. He made you see that every scene had a conflict and without a conflict you cannot have a scene. That is the essence of theater of conflict. So you understand your place within the framework of the scene—and that you have an objective.

As an actor, Lee Grant learned her trade in theater. She performed in plays written by the world's great playwrights. She also sang and danced in musicals. She has performed in almost 100 movie, stage, and television roles.

In 1951, she was cast as a shoplifter in the film version of *Detective Story*. Grant was nominated for an Academy Award for best supporting actress and won the award for best actress at the 1952 Cannes Film Festival. She says:

> My whole way of looking at myself and the theater was not to push to play leads. I wanted to play the small parts. I didn't want to push up front. I wanted a long-lived career. I had an instinct very early about what it meant to be raised and adored. It was a shock to get all those awards for a little bitty part I was hiding in.

Grant's acting career ran into a roadblock after *Detective Story*. She was blacklisted—primarily because she was married to a blacklisted Hollywood writer named Arnold Manoff.

Although she could not work in Hollywood, Grant continued to do plays in New York. She also taught acting. It was a step that would lead her down the road to directing. "It was teaching that really got me into directing. Because when you're teaching, you're concentrating on other people and their work," she explains.

By the 1960s, Grant was no longer blacklisted, and she worked again as an actor. She was in demand for a number of major films. In 1975, she appeared in a film called *Shampoo*, playing the role of an upscale suburbanite housewife having an affair with her hairdresser, played by Warren Beatty. Her performance won her an Academy Award.

A Directing Career

At about this time, Lee Grant received a call from the American Film Institute. They were starting a program to train women directors and asked if she could recommend any. Grant suggested a few women and then asked, "Well, what about me?"

Grant was accepted into the program and soon directed her first feature. It was a film based on a play by Swedish writer Johan Strindberg called *The Father*. She rounded up a number of her friends and shot it in an old castle over a long weekend. It was considered one the best works done at the institute. But despite its excellence, Grant could not get any work.

Then, in 1980, Grant made a documentary called *The Willmar 8*. She explains:

> I learned about these eight women who had worked in a bank in Willmar, Minnesota, and who were picketing the bank for unfair treatment despite the bitter-cold winter weather. For years they had trained men to do certain jobs and the men were then promoted and paid more while the women remained at the same level. They sued the bank for discrimination and eventually lost. But their struggle deeply impressed me and eventually it did help other women win their battles for equal treatment.

Her next big project was a feature film based on a book by Tillie Olsen, *Tell Me a Riddle*. In the film, an older couple revive their relationship as death approaches. "That was a book that was very close to me," Grant explains. "I was so tied in with that yearning for revolution that [the wife] had. At the same time, it was a love story. And it gave me

Lee Grant (right) with Tillie Olsen, author of Tell Me a Riddle

an extraordinary chance to show love and passion between two old people."

Grant believed that once she proved that she could make a successful feature film, a new career would begin for her in Hollywood. Says Grant:

> I thought the doors would open to me as a director. But nobody at the studios would give me a picture to direct. . . . I was horrified that I, a beloved actress—and I was beloved; I had so many awards—couldn't be given a feature film. When I asked for a chance to direct, the studio chiefs looked at me as if I had belched in public. They were shocked.
>
> Today, there are a growing number of women directors who not only make good films, but whose films make money for the studios, which is of course their main interest. My problem is that there's not a market for the kind of films I want to make.

In 1982, Grant gave up her life in Hollywood and returned to New York with her second husband, Joseph Feury, then a director of commercials. They formed a production company, and Grant concentrated on her directing career. She began making documentaries for the HBO cable network.

In 1986, Grant made a film for HBO on homelessness called *Down and Out in America*. She exposed the contradiction between the country's wealth and the plight of the homeless. *Down and Out* won an Academy Award. Lee Grant then went on to direct a feature film for television based on the documentary. "It's a world of difference working between the two. The documentary is so open and improvisational. Features are so rigidly formulated and thought out. I was pleased with both," Grant says.

In 1987, Grant won the Director's Guild of America Award for *Nobody's Child*. In the feature film, a young girl mistakenly diagnosed as schizophrenic is forced to spend many years in an institution. "I was really pleased to win that award because it meant that my fellow directors considered my film the best made that year. I couldn't believe it," she says.

Grant feels that a key to her success is that she approaches making a movie for television and an independent film for theaters in the same way. She also works with talented camera operators. "I always went for great cameramen," says Grant. "I watched programs made by the British Broadcasting Corporation for British television. The quality of the photography—as well as the programs—was far above ours."

Today, Grant is directing a series of biographical portraits for Lifetime TV. "It's a great opportunity for me," she explains. "It gives me the chance to meet almost all the women I've been intrigued by. To sit down and ask any questions I want to, to probe and find out why they have done what they did." Among

Lee Grant directs a television documentary on breast cancer in 1997.

the women she has done stories about are Vanessa Redgrave, Lauren Bacall, Gloria Steinem, and Margot Kidder.

Grant has recently finished a documentary about gun control, a subject that deeply concerns her. She feels a great responsibility with her documentaries. She explains:

> When I made a film on homelessness, it was because I wanted to help eradicate homelessness. When I made a film on breast cancer, it was to help eradicate breast cancer. And the film I am making now, with my own money, on gun control is because I want to eradicate handguns and the violence to which they contribute. I want my films to make a difference.

Chapter Six

Sam Pollard: Editing—The Heart of the Matter

When director Spike Lee called Sam Pollard to edit the film *Mo' Better Blues*, his son was impressed. "Wow, you're going to take it, aren't you?" he asked. But Pollard was cautious about working with the country's best-known African-American movie director.

Pollard was the first member of his family to go to college. "Until the 1960s, my father made and sold tablecloths for a living. In 1964, he was able to get a civil service job as a housing caretaker and remained in that job until he retired," explains Pollard. Although Pollard's family did not try to push him into a specific career, they impressed on him the need to make a living.

In junior high school, Sam Pollard took a test to get into Charles Evans Hughes High School, which had a special electrical engineering program. He passed the test and was admitted. After a year of taking mathematics and physics courses, his teachers told him he didn't have the aptitude for engineering. So Pollard transferred to a regular liberal arts program. Was he disappointed? "Not at all," he says laughing. "In fact, I was relieved."

SAM POLLARD

Profession: Producer, director, and editor

Year; place of birth: 1950; New York, New York

Education: B.A., Baruch College

Mailing address: c/o Undergraduate Film and TV Department, New York University, 721 Broadway, New York, NY 10012

Career accomplishments: Coproduced and edited the Academy Award–nominated *4 Little Girls* and has edited several Spike Lee films

Selected films (as editor unless noted): *Bamboozled* (2000), *4 Little Girls* (1998, coproducer and editor), *Clockers* (1994), *Jungle Fever* (1991), and *Mo' Better Blues* (1990)

Words of wisdom: "An editor has the ability to create a world and express a truth based on the belief that we have something important to say that we want to share with our audiences."

"The one class I really liked was history," he says. "European history. American history. I did really well in those classes. I enjoyed being like an archaeologist—digging up the past to find out what happened back then." Another course that captured Pollard's imagination was English literature. He read Charles Dickens, Mark Twain, and F. Scott Fitzgerald. Ernest Hemingway was one of his favorites.

As Sam Pollard was coming of age in high school, the world about him was undergoing radical change. Tens of thousands of young people around the country were demonstrating against racial segregation in the South and against the Vietnam War. As a black youth, Pollard found his own identity in black writers such as Langston Hughes, James Baldwin, and Amiri Baraka.

After graduating from high school, Pollard wanted to make sure that he chose something that would lead to a steady job.

In college, Pollard majored in marketing research. As much as he liked it, he felt unfulfilled:

> One day, I went to see my counselor seeking an outlet. I told her that I was looking for something else to do to take my mind off of these horrid statistics classes. She asked me what I liked to do. I said, "I like to read a lot and go to the movies." My mother was a big movie fan. She asked if I was curious about how movies are made. I said, "Not really." She said she knew about a workshop that had just been created at the local public television station, Channel 13. Its goal was to try and get more African-Americans behind the camera.

Pollard reluctantly decided to give it a chance. He thought that the only way to see if it interested him was to tie it to his marketing class. "I was the only person in this class of twenty-five people who was interested in movies from a business perspective," he says.

One of Pollard's first assignments was to work as an assistant camera operator. His job was to take the film from the can and load it into the camera magazine. Because film cannot be exposed to light, this process has to be carried out in complete darkness. Pollard had to put the unopened film can and the camera magazine in a black changing bag and seal the bag. Without being able to see, he had to place his hands inside the bag, remove the film from the can, open the camera magazine, and place the film inside. The process intimidated Pollard. "I was so terrified of making a mistake, I said, 'I can't do this.' So they made me an editor instead," he explains.

Becoming an Editor

Editing is the process of cutting and rearranging all the different footage that has been shot. In a feature film, the footage is usually based on a script. The script's scenes are broken down into shots—a long shot, a medium shot, a close-up, a pan (side to side), a tilt (up and down), a zoom (in and out), or a tracking shot. An editor may receive as many as thirty or forty takes of a single scene. The director and the editor select the best shots. Then the editor puts together the shots to create the scene and the story in the script.

Editing for a documentary is much different. The footage may be of several different scenes, many of which may not have been planned. The editor must take this footage and make it conform to the director's vision of the documentary.

When Sam Pollard learned to edit, he had to learn how to join pieces of film physically to create a scene. Today, videotape has replaced film in most editing rooms and, while the principles are the same, editing is done electronically on a computer or a video-editing machine.

Pollard's first task was to learn how to cut the film together using editing equipment. Pollard explains:

Sam Pollard working at a computer with an editing system

> What really turned me on was that if I made a mistake, if I spliced two pieces of film together and didn't like the cut, I could undo the splice and nobody would know I made the mistake. It was like a miracle. I got so excited about this, I really felt I wanted to get into editing.

In the summer of 1972, Pollard got a job in marketing. Two weeks later, a call came from a production manager on a feature. They were looking for an apprentice editor. Was he interested? Pollard traveled to the suburbs of New York for an interview. He was offered the job—if he would agree to drive the footage they shot to the laboratory in New York at the end of each day. But Pollard couldn't drive! He went back to marketing. One week later, they called again. They had not been able to find an assistant editor willing to drive. Was Pollard still interested?

The picture was called *Ganja & Hess*, which Pollard describes as an "intellectual horror film." His job was relatively menial, but it allowed him to learn about editing. He worked on the film during the day and attended marketing classes at night.

One day, the editor asked Pollard to move a shot from one spot to another while the editor went to lunch. He says:

> The machine was very complicated. If you lost control of it, it would be a disaster. Needless to say, I lost control. I let the machine rip the first thirty scenes right down the middle. I thought, "This is it. I am going to be fired." I spent my whole lunch hour trying to repair the damage. When the editor returned from lunch, I confessed what I did. To my surprise, he didn't fire me. He said, "Everybody makes mistakes."

Gradually, Pollard learned not to make mistakes, and he developed more skills. By 1973, ready to graduate from college, he was faced with a major decision. Should he pursue his original career in marketing or take a job as an assistant editor? He talked it over with his parents. His mother said to him, "You've got to do what you think is best."

As soon as he graduated, Pollard went to work as an assistant to a first-rate editor named Victor Kanefsky. Because Kanefsky had another editing job, he turned the film over to Pollard. "Victor would give me the notes on how to cut a particular scene. He would explain why he put it together one way rather than another. In this way I learned how to edit," explains Pollard.

After working like this for several years, Pollard was given the chance to edit his first film by himself. "I was the editor, the assistant, and the apprentice all wound into one," he says.

Pollard worked hard to make sure that he was making the best possible cut. In addition to editing the picture, he had to prepare all the sound tracks. During the editing process, the sound is divided into a number of different tracks. Music may be on one track, sound effects on another, a narrator on a third, and people's voices on a fourth. Once the separate tracks are completed, the editor must then take them to a sound studio, where they are mixed into one final track.

Two weeks before the mixing session, Pollard was working until 4 A.M. seven days a week. He explains:

> The night before the mix, at midnight, I was so exhausted, I couldn't make it. I broke down in tears. At 12:30 in the morning, I called a friend who was an editor and told him I was in a crisis and needed help. He came over and the two of us worked all night getting the film ready for the mix. By morning, the tracks were barely ready. At the end of the mix, the technician turned to me and gently asked, "Have you ever thought about getting into another line of work?"

After that baptism by fire, Pollard was hired as an editor for a program called *3-2-1 Contact*. It was a popular science show for children that aired on the PBS television network during the 1980s. He says of this major step forward in his career:

> I was very competitive. I looked at every editor's work and studied how they cut the show together. I asked an editor whose work I respected to come and look at my cut so that I could improve it. It was about this time that I had my worst experience as an editor. I worked for a guy who was a very good filmmaker, but was very sarcastic and difficult to work for. I finally had an argument with him and quit. He asked me to come back but I wouldn't.

Pollard then went to California to work on low-budget features. He worked on some films and learned a lot there. Then a friend told him that Henry Hampton, the director and producer of the classic documentary *Eyes on the Prize* which traces the history of the civil rights movement of the 1960s, was about to start a sequel. He was looking for a producer for two of the shows. Pollard agreed to coproduce. He says:

> Now that I had to do it myself, I realized it wasn't so easy to be a producer. My job as editor was an easy job. Producers had to come up with the concept for the show and how to execute it. Henry would also ask us, "What is the story?" He would say, "If it doesn't excite me, you're not doing your job."

A Call From Spike Lee

One evening, while Pollard was relaxing at home with his children, the phone rang. His son answered and came into the room with an astonished look on his face. "Dad, it's Spike Lee," he said. Lee was then an up-and-coming feature director about to start production on a film called *Mo' Better Blues*. Someone had recommended Pollard to him as an editor. To his son's astonishment, Pollard turned Lee down because of another commitment.

A month later Lee called again. Again, Pollard said he couldn't do it. Finally the two of them met. "We talked for an hour. That is, I talked. Spike hardly said a word. At the end of the hour, I said I would do it. I worked things out with Henry

Hampton on *Eyes on the Prize* and then went to New York," explains Jersey.

Usually, in feature filmmaking, the editor begins putting the film together as each day's scenes are shot, sent to the lab, and developed. As a result, by the time the film is completed, a first assembly is also completed. But Spike Lee did not work that way with Pollard. Pollard explains:

> Two weeks into the shooting, after we've been screening dailies every night, I asked Spike, "When do you want to start cutting?" Spike said, "I don't want you to cut anything." I was surprised. Another week goes by. Again I asked, "What do you want me to cut?" He doesn't want me to cut anything. Fourth week goes by. Fifth week. Sixth week. I begin to realize that he doesn't trust me.
>
> Twelve weeks go by and I haven't cut a thing even though I'm being paid. The shooting is finally over and I say, "What do you want me to cut?" Again he says, "I don't want you to cut anything. I'm going away for a week. Don't do anything." I'm fit to be tied. He goes away and comes back. And then he wants to see all the dailies again in order of the film. We go over them again and preselect. We would look at a scene, go over the notes, then he would tell me to cut. Then we would look at the next scene, go over the notes we had already made, and I would cut it. That's how we cut *Mo' Better Blues*. We cut the film and I figure I'm not going to work for this guy anymore.
>
> After the film is over, he asks me to cut his next film *Jungle Fever*. Two weeks into the film, he tells me to start cutting.

Spike Lee asked Pollard to work on his next film, *Malcolm X*, which was based on the biography by Alex Haley. Pollard says:

> I wanted to but I was also afraid of being known as "Spike Lee's editor." I was editing long before Spike Lee became Spike Lee. And I didn't want to be pigeonholed. Anyhow,

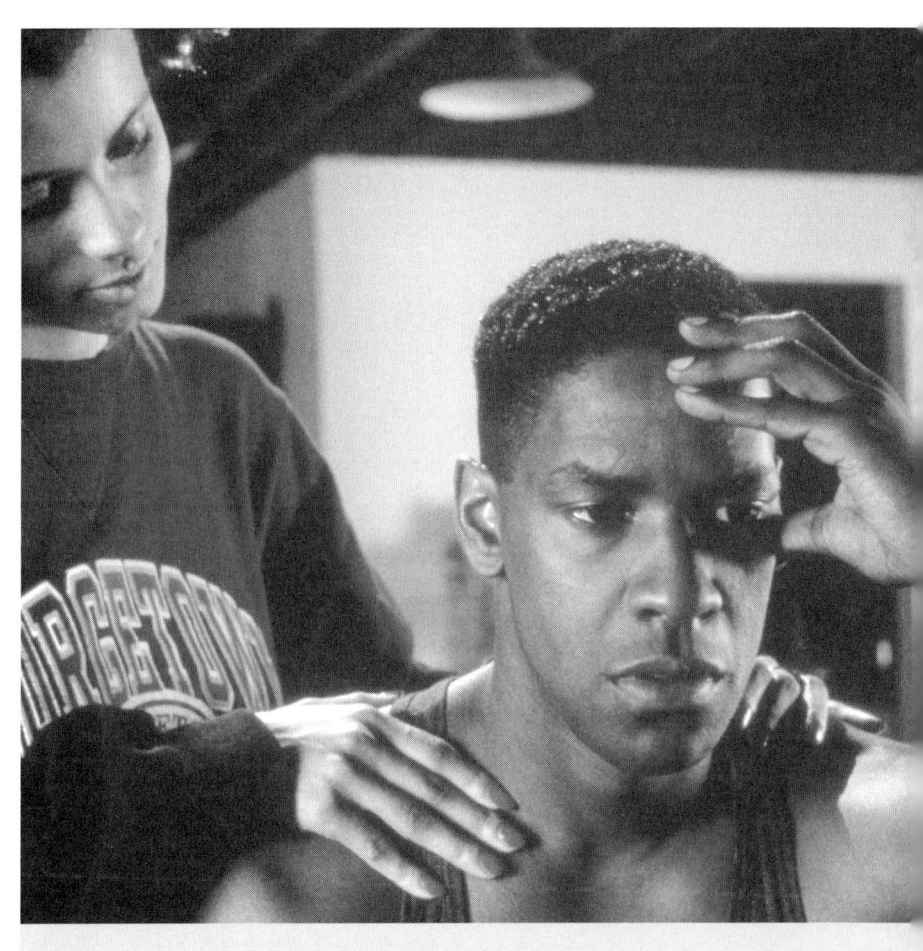

A still from Mo' Better Blues, *starring Academy Award–winner Denzel Washington (right)*

I agreed to do it, but at the same time, I was offered the chance to make a documentary I wanted to make. For a while, I tried to do both jobs, but I felt that I couldn't do justice to *Malcolm*. I finally went to Spike and told him that I would have to quit. I told him that the documentary was important to me. Everybody said I was crazy to walk off such an important film.

Pollard felt sure that his days with Spike Lee were finished. But two years later, Lee called him to edit *Clockers*, a film he was making based on the best-selling novel. Pollard was hesitant. He explains: "When Spike saw my hesitation, he asked me if I had a problem working with him. I told him no, but that what I really wanted was to produce his first documentary film with him." Lee agreed.

During this period, Pollard began teaching film courses at New York University. He emphasizes to his students that they must learn how to edit to be a filmmaker:

> Editing to me is the heart of the process. It teaches you about the rhythm and pacing of a film. It teaches you how to structure a film and tell a story with images. Computers have made it possible for almost anyone to learn editing. They make it possible for anyone who wants to become a filmmaker to realize his or her dreams.

In 1994, Sam Pollard and Spike Lee produced the Academy Award–nominated *4 Little Girls*. The film concerned the bombing of a black church in 1963 in Birmingham, Alabama, in which four black children were killed. The bomb was planted by members of the Ku Klux Klan. Only one man had been convicted of the crime and sent to prison. A second man had died in the 1980s. Two other prime suspects were never arrested, even though one of them had boasted about what he had done.

In 2000, however, the two suspects were indicted for murder. Pollard says:

> I would like to think that the film Spike and I made had something to do with the men being arrested. It's more than just coincidence I think that two main suspects had walked around free for over thirty-five years and that, only after our film came out, were they finally arrested and charged. As a filmmaker, I want to make a difference. I don't

Director Spike Lee interviews David Vann, the former mayor of Birmingham, Alabama, in 4 Little Girls. *Sam Pollard produced the documentary with Lee and edited the film.*

only want to entertain or educate an audience. I want to change the country into a better place for all people to live.

Today, Sam Pollard continues to produce and edit. He recently edited the Spike Lee film *Bamboozled*. Says Pollard:

> I have been editing for twenty-eight years and my love for it has not diminished. I enjoy the challenge of sitting with the material and coming up with a story by manipulating picture and sound. I still find the process mystical and magical.

Chapter Seven

Stephanie Black: Creating Documentaries and Music Videos

Stephanie Black's father may have started her love affair with film with his passion for James Bond films, but he certainly never intended his daughter to make a career out of it. "My father had his own love for the movies. He used to take us children at a very young age to special James Bond triple features, which he really enjoyed. But he didn't consider a degree in filmmaking as an option for a profession. It wasn't considered practical," explains Black.

At the State University of New York at Binghamton, Black was an environmental-science major, but filmmaking was her passion: "I would take my biology classes, my chemistry classes, my botany classes, and then run to sit in on film classes given by Ken Jacobs."

Jacobs is an experimental filmmaker whose films are noted for innovative visual techniques. He had a large influence on Black. Says Black, "I think it's important when you're young to have an individual who becomes a role model for you."

Stephanie Black remembers her first film:

> It was exciting to see the footage come back from the laboratory and find that, yes, I had exposed it properly and

STEPHANIE BLACK

Profession: Producer and director

Place of birth: Brooklyn, New York

Education: B.A., State University of New York at Binghamton

Web site for additional information: *lifeanddebt.org*

Career accomplishments: Won awards for the best documentary and best cinematography for *H-2 Worker* at the 1990 Sundance Film Festival and has directed a music video for Ziggy Marley

Selected films (as producer and director unless noted): *Life and Debt* (2001), *Making of Chant Down Babylon* (1999), and *Many Are Called, Few Are Chosen* (1992)

Words of wisdom: "The reason I love to do music videos with reggae artists is that I love the music and I love the artists. There's not big money in it, but there is artistic freedom."

---

that the images I had, until then, only seen through the viewfinder of my camera were actually there! It blew my mind. When I began to edit the film, joining one piece of film to the next, I was even more excited to discover that the idea that had been in my head was actually there on film. It was very thrilling for me. You never forget the first time you discover filmmaking.

After finishing college, Black decided she would go to Paris for the filmmaking courses she had wanted take as an undergraduate. There she was exposed to the works and style of many European filmmakers. She returned to New York resolved to become a filmmaker.

In New York, Black worked for a city program called Operation Green Thumb, whose goal was to beautify vacant city lots with vegetable gardens. But her heart was still in films. She signed up for a course in cinema studies at New York University. She says:

> It was good for me to be with film students from other countries who were extremely talented and very committed to becoming filmmakers. Each had their own way of using film and some have since have gone on to become successful filmmakers in Europe.
>
> At that time, I thought I wanted to make environmentally oriented films because I was coming from an environmental background. I had worked for environmental organizations, mixing my passion for films and environmental work.

Winning Her First Grant

While at NYU, Black competed for a grant offered by the American Can Company to make a film on hunger in America. She wrote a proposal for a film on a Mexican migrant farmworker and her family. Black won a $10,000 grant. She explains:

> I thought $10,000 was the most money in the world. It seemed like $10 million. I had met this family I wanted to film in Ohio, and when they went to Florida to work, I followed them there. I lived with them and went through a lot with them. But I could not get on the inside of their daily experience because I didn't speak Spanish and they didn't speak English.

So Black took a crash course in Spanish. During the class, she met a Haitian minister at a union meeting who had heard of her film project. He invited her to visit a camp where seasonal sugarcane workers from Jamaica lived during the harvest season. "I saw urine dripping from the ceiling, 2,500 radios blasting, and the men were lethargic, their faces glazed with despair," Black says.

Every year, sugar corporations in Florida import 10,000 workers, mostly from Jamaica, where unemployment is extremely high, to cut sugarcane in the fields. They come on a temporary visa, an H-2 as it is called. The work is backbreaking and brutal. They cut the cane with machetes under the hot sun while looking out for poisonous snakes. They wear shin guards to protect their legs from machete cuts. They are expected to cut 1 1/2 tons of cane per hour.

For the next three and a half years, Black documented the story of the cane cutters, which she called *H-2 Worker*. She sneaked into their living quarters and filmed the urine dripping onto the men as they slept. The men slept on narrow bunks as if they were in prison. The furniture was made of cardboard crates, and the rooms had little if any light.

Stephanie Black (right) filming H-2 Worker

When she wasn't filming, Black was trying to raise funds. "Like most independent filmmakers, you spend a lot of time searching for foundations to help finance the film. You write proposals, you arrange screenings, and then you wait. I supported myself by working as a proofreader at night, between 2 A.M. and 6 A.M.," she explains.

Black was lucky. Her project received around $140,000 in grants, though that is not a large amount for an hour-long film.

While making the film, Black had to be careful. She was not allowed official access to the camps. As far as the sugar companies were concerned, the camps were off limits to most people. She explains:

> I had to evade the police and the sugar-company officials in order to enter the camps. I was more scared of the cops than of anyone else. We rented a new car every couple of days so that the police would not recognize the same license plates every time we were there and hopefully wouldn't stop us. Whenever they did see us filming, I'd say we were taking pictures for postcards or we were in Florida visiting my grandmother—or anything else that suddenly came to mind. I'm sure being a woman made it easier for me than if a man had tried to make the film.

Another problem Black had to deal with was protecting the privacy of the workers she interviewed. "They were afraid that if someone saw them talking to me, they would be reported to their bosses and sent home," Black says. "We would arrange it so that the worker walked down the road of the camp alone before we picked him up. Then we'd go somewhere and shoot and then bring him back to a place where he could walk into camp alone."

The film had a powerful impact in the United States and was widely reviewed. Senator Edward Kennedy of Massachusetts and several other U.S. senators sponsored a congressional screening of the film. It was also shown at a number of film festivals, including the Sundance Film Festival, where it won awards for best documentary and best cinematography. Black hopes that the H-2 program will be changed so that "when the cane cutters return to Florida, they will not be working under the same conditions."

The World of Music Videos

Stephanie Black also found another filmmaking channel through which she could express her social concerns—music videos. At first, it might seem that music videos are far removed from social documentaries. But Black is fortunate to have found some creative freedom in making music videos. Her work combines her passion for social justice with her love of music.

Black has learned music video business can be complex and quite commercial, however. She explains:

> The record companies produce videos, which the artists ultimately pay for out of their royalties, in order to publicize the artist. They want to see the videos played on MTV in order to be seen by as large an audience as possible. You have to make a music video strong enough so that the station will show it, which also means you have to know what MTV is showing. A lot of videos get made but never get played. Or they get played on smaller stations like BET or local cable channels. It often depends on the budget for the video and who the artist is.

Stephanie Black became a music video director after a call from Elektra Records. People at the record company had seen *H-2 Workers* and were considering matching her with a singer named KRS-One for his new album of hip-hop and reggae. Black describes the scene: "I was totally nervous at the first meeting and said very little. I wanted to do it and I wanted to do well, but I had no experience with music videos. I got the job and we shot in Washington Square, a small park in New York."

Directing music videos can be as challenging as directing a film. Here, Eurythmics singer Annie Lennox is filmed on the set of the MTV Music Video Award–nominated video for "Missionary Man."

Some record companies only work with well-known directors. Others are looking for new talent. Record companies ask directors for a two- or three-page treatment for a particular song and look at the director's reel before making a final decision. The treatment spells out to the record company the style and feel of the video. Black says:

> So you listen to the song over and over again, become familiar with the artist, and then write your approach to the video for that song. You try to describe the mood and look of the video, and the story line if the video is going to tell a story.

When a director is selected, he or she is informed about the changes needed in the treatment. "Music videos are a business. There's a core of talented music-video directors who may have freedom of control but most directors have to follow the requirements of a record company," Black says.

If the budget is large enough, the shoot might last a week. A small budget might limit a director to one day's shooting. No matter what the budget, the sound is never recorded live. Black explains:

> You play a track of the song and the singer mouths the words as if he or she is singing. You film enough to cover the song and to have all the shots you need. I always try to use dancers because I love dance and they add a lot of energy and vitality to the video.

Many young filmmakers will sometimes make an extremely low-budget music video for the experience. One of the rewards is working with the artists. Black enjoys working with talented musicians:

> Working with artists I respect is like living out a fantasy I had when I was sixteen. Some artists are so extraordinary to work with, they make you raise your work a notch. When the artists trust the director they're working with, it's a great collaboration.

While a director's imagination may be unlimited, what eventually limits the video is the budget. At times, a music company may spend as little as $15,000 for a video. A more common figure is between $60,000 and $250,000. A big-budget video for someone like Madonna or Michael Jackson might cost as much as $1 million.

While Black concentrates on the creative side of making music videos, a producer is responsible for the organization and finances of the project. The producer's responsibility is to see that the video is made within budget and on time. Black says that when she creates a video, she must be sure that the budget allows her to realize her ideas. She says:

You're always making trade-offs. You may have a great idea to shoot on top of the crater of a volcano, but unless you can afford to take the band there, you'll have settle for a more affordable location somewhere else. Or you might have a great idea for a shot but it will take five hours to do and you only have enough money for one day's shooting for the whole video.

Some beginning music-video makers must work as producer and director. They may try to save costs by using inexpensive consumer equipment such as Super 8 and digital video, or they may shoot in locations where little or no artificial light is needed and get friends to work for them without pay or at reduced rates. Black feels that the key to a good music video relies as much on the technology as on good visual and musical performances from the band. Postproduction can create dazzling special effects.

Another attraction for Black about music videos is that they can allow her to incorporate a social statement as part of the video's content and style. One of her music videos was shot in Jamaica with a reggae singer named Anthony B. The song was called "Mr. Heartless." "The song was about how the greed of our society destroys the dreams and lives of children," Black explains. She says:

> In making the video, I first wanted to be absolutely faithful to the song. I looked for visual counterparts that would symbolically show the destruction of children's lives to match the mood and lyrics of the song.
>
> When I discovered that every morning children in Kingston hitched rides to the dump by hanging on to garbage trucks so they could rummage through the refuse for things they could sell, I knew I had the location that would best express the song. We shot the video in this setting because the lyrics of the song lent themselves to it. And we intercut these scenes with images of young children playing violins and dancing to show what the potential of

these young people is and how it is lost because they are condemned to the dump by this greedy society.

While some directors have reported occasional difficulties with rock groups, Stephanie Black has had only good experiences. She says:

> Almost everyone I have worked with has been very professional and fun. Loving their music helps a lot. And while I will always make social documentaries, I will continue to make music videos.
>
> I would love to have the opportunity to make a video for Tracy Chapman. I love her work. Her songs are about things I care about. They're beautiful and express very deep feelings about people and their sufferings and concerns.

Today

In 2001, Stephanie Black produced and directed *Life and Debt*. This searing documentary shares the stories of individual Jamaicans and looks at the effect of international lending on Jamaica's economy. Black incorporates excerpts from the work

A still from Stephanie Black's Life and Debt, *a documentary shot in Jamaica*

of award-winning writer Jamaica Kincaid. *The New Yorker* called the documentary "a comprehensive and involving film about the pillaging of a beautiful island and its people."

Whether she is raising money for her next project or directing music videos, filmmaking keeps Black busy. During her time in Jamaica, she even produced several documentary segments for the PBS children's program *Sesame Street*!

What advice would this energetic filmmaker offer young people? Hands-on experience is vital, according to Black. For those who seek to make a career as a filmmaker, Stephanie Black advises going to film school:

> If a young person asks me how they could get into the music-video business, there are books they can read and Web sites they can visit. But I would advise them to go to a film school to learn how to make films. If I hadn't gone to film school, I would have been just another person thinking about film ideas. In film schools they put a camera in your hand. You have to use it. If you don't, you're going to fail the class. Then it just becomes natural for you to use the camera.

Chapter Eight

Norman Jewison: A Hollywood Director Follows His Dream

Long before Norman Jewison became one of Hollywood's top movie directors, Jewison ran his own little movie theater. He explains:

> I grew up during the Great Depression of the 1930s. When I was about eight or nine years old, I got a little movie projector that would run short 8-millimeter film reels, which were used to distribute movies in the days before videocassettes were invented. You had to crank the projector by hand, and if you didn't keep the film moving, the bulb, which was extremely hot, would burn the film. I would get several of the three- to four-minute action or adventure films they put out in those days—Westerns, that sort of thing. I would invite the neighborhood kids to see the movies and I would charge them one penny a piece. I would project the film onto a white sheet. When I had enough pennies, then I would go see a real movie.

Jewison grew up in a working-class section of Toronto, Ontario. His parents owned a dry-goods store in which there was a post office. Because his parents worked long hours, he spent

NORMAN JEWISON

Profession: Director and producer

Year; place of birth: 1926; Toronto, Ontario, Canada

Education: B.A., Victoria College, University of Toronto

Mailing address: c/o Canadian Film Centre, Windfields, 2489 Bayview Avenue, Toronto, Ontario, Canada M2L 1A8

Career accomplishments: Has received twelve Academy Awards, including the prestigious Irving G. Thalberg Memorial Award

Selected films (as director and producer unless noted): *The Hurricane* (1999), *Moonstruck* (1987), *Agnes of God* (1987), *A Soldier's Story* (1984), *Jesus Christ Superstar* (1973, director, producer, and writer), *Fiddler on the Roof* (1971), *The Thomas Crown Affair* (1968), *In the Heat of the Night* (1967, director), and *The Cincinnati Kid* (1965, director)

Words of wisdom: "Never give up on your dream. Stay committed and passionate. Try to remain confident and positive. Be honest and always seek the truth."

a lot of time alone. Movies were a way of escaping into a fantasy world. "I never dreamed of making movies for a career," Jewison explains. "They were my favorite form of entertainment, an escape from the real world into a fantasy world. Sitting there in a darkened room, I was gone."

During World War II, Jewison enlisted in the Canadian navy at the age of seventeen. At the war's end, he took his first trip to the United States. He traveled into the South.

Jewison encountered things there he had never seen before. He couldn't understand why black people couldn't ride in the same section of the bus as whites or drink from the same water fountain. "It was my first exposure to racism and I was shocked," he explains. "Black soldiers were asked to serve their country, and give their lives if necessary, and yet they were treated like this. I couldn't understand how white people could think that way." Witnessing this injustice engraved itself in Jewison's psyche and eventually resurfaced in some of his best work.

After his trip to the United States, Norman Jewison went to the University of Toronto to study English and philosophy. He also studied piano and music theory at the Royal Conservatory. Then television changed his life. "I knew that it would be the greatest medium of communication ever devised," he says.

A Start in Directing

Using his last few dollars, Jewison went to England, where he worked for the BBC, the British Broadcasting Corporation. He worked as a writer and actor, learning the new medium while barely earning enough to eat.

Then he was invited to Canada to participate in the newly formed television program at the Canadian Broadcasting Company (CBC). Jewison worked at a variety of jobs until he eventually directed. He soon became one of the network's top directors. When the William Morris Agency, then the most powerful talent agency in the United States, saw his work, his career as a director in America was launched.

Jewison directed television shows for the popular *Your Hit Parade* in the 1950s. He directed a number of the biggest stars of the day—Judy Garland, Frank Sinatra, Jackie Gleason, and Danny Kaye.

One of his most satisfying television shows was *Tonight With Belafonte*, starring African-American actor and singer Harry Belafonte. The show was broadcast during a dangerous time, when racial tension in the country was extremely high. Jewison recalls, "During rehearsals, Belafonte was on the phone all the time to Louisiana. It was intense because schools were being integrated for the first time as mobs of whites surrounded them in protest. We were all worried."

The show, broadcast live, was a hit. In the South, however, twenty-six stations refused to show it. In Birmingham, Alabama, protestors blocked the broadcast of the program by throwing chains across the transmission lines. The show won an Emmy Award, television's highest honor. It was one of three such awards that Jewison would eventually win.

Jewison felt that the early days of television were a highly creative period. Because nobody was really familiar with the medium, a great deal of experimentation took place. Some of America's most creative talent worked together to produce entertaining and well-crafted programs. Television became so popular that many film studios were afraid that it would eventually replace movies.

When the networks began using ratings to decide how much to charge advertisers, their objectives became mass audiences rather than quality programming. As television became increasingly popular and reached a wider audience, advertising agencies exerted greater influence on the shows and their content. Jewison, like many of his colleagues, began to regard the movie industry as the place to use their creative talents.

In 1957, Jewison got his first opportunity to direct a film. He explains:

> Tony Curtis had been watching my shows and asked if I would like to direct a movie he wanted to make. He asked me if I would read a script. It was called *40 Pounds of Trouble*, a comedy based on a famous short story called "Little Miss Marker," about a gambler who finds himself taking care of a little girl for business reasons and suddenly discovers his life filled with unexpected complications. I told Tony I was a television director, not a movie director. Tony asked me to read the script anyhow.

Jewison agreed to do the film. By doing so, he entered a whole new world. Making a feature for Hollywood is different from working in television. "It was a much slower process. In television I used three cameras to record a scene in three different angles at the same time. In film, you work with just one camera and have to set up each angle separately," he explains.

The Varied Work of a Director

For Jewison, like many directors, the film begins months before shooting. He first works on the script with the writer to ensure that the story is structured properly, that the characters are well drawn, and that the picture can be made within the budget. "Every picture has to have a point," he says. "It must be clear to the director what the movie is about." This means that each line of dialogue, scene, and sequence must move the story along.

Jewison also discusses the preproduction process with his key production personnel. He says:

> You have to rely on the people you're working with. No director can be camera operator, editor, set designer, and writer all in one. You hire people who can bring their own creativity to a film, which will make your film better and bring solutions to problems that you might not have thought of.

Jewison discusses with the director of photography how the film will be shot. He reviews the locations that production personnel have scouted, discusses casting with talent agents, reviews the actors' wardrobes, and meets with art directors. If special effects such as gunfire or spaceships are needed, the director must communicate his or her vision with the visual-effects specialists.

Rehearsal is often an important part of the preproduction process. It is the director's responsibility to help the actor find the emotional truth of his or her character before shooting starts. A script, for all its brilliance, is at best a skeleton for the film. The actor gives it life and blood. "Some actors are very good at giving you the externals of the character. They have all the right moves, all the right facial expressions, and the right intonations of the lines. But their inner life is missing. This is one reason why the rehearsals are so important," says Jewison.

Rehearsals take place with the director and the actors before shooting begins. Jewison explains:

I like rehearsing actors, especially actors who like rehearsals. I remember when I did a picture called *And Justice for All* with Al Pacino. Pacino likes to rehearse. He loves acting and his acting gets better as he rehearses. He's also a perfectionist on the set.

In one scene he played with another actor—Jack Warden—Pacino was not satisfied with his performance. We did the scene twenty-six times and each time Warden had to eat a chicken salad sandwich. By the last take, Warden was so fed up with chicken salad sandwiches that he threatened, "One more take and I'm out of here."

The scenes in a film script are usually filmed out of order. All the scenes that take place in one location are generally filmed at the same time and then the crew moves to the next location. So an actor may find himself doing scenes from different parts of the script at the same location. The director will also ask the actor to repeat the same scene several times from different camera angles. If the actor is not getting the lines right—or is making mistakes—the director must reshoot the scene.

The director must make sure that the actors maintain an emotional energy consistent with the film in sequence. Solid rehearsal in sequence before shooting begins helps actors jump around in time and maintain their emotional energy and the character's state of mind. That preparation gives them the security of knowing where they are in the time frame of the story emotionally, physically, and mentally.

In making a film, Jewison also works very closely with his camera operator. They plan the lighting, camera angles, and camera moves for each scene. The director and camera operator also choreograph, or block, the actors' movements for each scene.

The most brilliant moves and lighting serve little purpose, however, if the director does not get good performances from the actors. One of Jewison's most satisfying films was *The Cincinnati Kid* (1965), starring Steve McQueen. The film was about poker players. McQueen played a young upstart who feels he is good enough to beat America's champion poker player. "*The Cincinnati Kid* was a film I really wanted to do. It made me feel good. There's a lot of me in it. And I surprised a lot of people who said you can't make a film about a card game," Jewison says.

At the time, Steve McQueen was one of Hollywood's biggest stars. Jewison felt like a kind of older brother to McQueen. He explains:

In 1965, Norman Jewison directed Steve McQueen in The Cincinnati Kid. *This still from the movie shows McQueen playing poker.*

We got along fine but a lot of the time I couldn't understand his slang. He was very hip. He'd say things like, "You know what's really important? Who's got the juice, man." He was so hip, I never knew what he was saying, but we became very close and I was very protective. I'd just look at him with a puzzled expression on my face. He was not a great actor but he was a movie star. The camera loved him. He was always believable in everything he did.

Films That Made an Impact

In the late 1960s, Jewison was given the opportunity to make a film he very much wanted to make. The civil rights movement was spreading all across the South. Young people, black and white, were breaking down the barriers of segregation while the U.S. Supreme Court declared, in decision after decision, that segregation was unconstitutional in every sphere of public life.

During this turbulent time, Norman Jewison received a script for a film called *In the Heat of the Night*, a racially explosive film for its time. It told the story of an African-American law-enforcement officer from Philadelphia on a visit to his family in the South and a prejudiced white sheriff, who reluctantly work together to solve a murder case. During the investigation, the two men develop a friendship and respect for one another.

The film caught the attention of many people, including the attorney general of the United States! Jewison explains:

> Before I started filming I was skiing with my children at Sun Valley, Idaho. I met Bobby Kennedy there, President Kennedy's brother, who was also there with his kids. I had the opportunity to discuss the project with him. He strongly urged me to do the film.
>
> "It's very important that you make this film now. Timing is everything," he said, "in politics, life, and art. This film is very important for this moment." He sent me interviews the Justice Department had taped with young African-American

students, books, and a lot of other material that he thought might be helpful.

Filming took place in southern Illinois. Jewison felt it was too risky to shoot the film in the South. Its stars were Sidney Poitier and Rod Steiger. He says:

> It was wonderful working with two brilliant actors like Rod Steiger and Sidney Poitier. They improvised one scene and it was great. The two of them began to reveal their loneliness to each other as law-enforcement officers, dis-

In 1967, Norman Jewison directs a young actor in a scene from the Academy Award–winning In the Heat of the Night.

covering what they had in common even though racial barriers divided them. Moments like this are one of the joys of filmmaking, when people you work with make unexpected contributions that help your film.

In the Heat of the Night won the Academy Award for best picture and Rod Steiger won an Academy Award for his performance. The picture won awards for writing, sound, and editing too. "I also won the New York Film Critics Award for the film and Robert Kennedy presented the award to me," Jewison recalls. "As he handed it to me, he whispered, 'See? I told you the timing was right.'"

After making *In the Heat of the Night,* Jewison turned to one of his favorite movie forms—the musical. He directed *Fiddler on the Roof,* the story of a Jewish family and community in nineteenth-century Russia affected by the historic changes of the time.

Musicals are difficult to direct because the singing has to be believable within the dramatic context of the story. "In *Fiddler,* there was a wedding scene in which a father sings a song about how shocked he is to realize his little girl has finally grown up. What makes the song work in the film is that we staged the scene at the wedding with the father watching the marriage take place. So the song comes across as if we are listening to the thoughts in his head," explains Jewison.

Norman Jewison viewed *Fiddler* as a kind of a homecoming: "When I was a kid, I encountered a lot of anti-Semitism. My name is *Jewison,* which I suppose some people could interpret to mean 'son of a Jew.' But I am not Jewish. I am English and Methodist. Yet, the other kids thought I was Jewish and persecuted me."

Fiddler on the Roof was a critical and commercial success. But the film reminded Jewison that despite the best planning, the director is not always in charge:

> The biggest problems come when you try to control life and the world. I remember that during the production of

Fiddler on the Roof we had a farewell scene between young lovers, which was supposed to take place in the snow. We planned to shoot the scene in Yugoslavia at a time of year when snow is always on the ground. Well, there always is snow, except for that one time when we were going to shoot that scene. Suddenly it was spring and, instead of snow, we had flowers blooming. We had to go back to London to shoot other dance scenes and then returned when we finally had snow.

Although Jewison continued to make comedies, racial issues continued to concern him. In 1984, he made *A Soldier's Story*, a film about the murder of a black sergeant at an army camp. The film was nominated for three Academy Awards.

And in 1999, Jewsion produced and directed *The Hurricane,* based on the true-life story of former middleweight boxing champion of the world Rubin "Hurricane" Carter. This African-American boxer and another man named John Artis were framed for murder by the New Jersey police and prosecutor's office. Carter spent nineteen years in prison before the federal courts ordered him released because the trial was racially prejudiced and evidence had been tampered with.

The injustice outraged Norman Jewison in much the same way injustice had outraged him during his first trip to the United States at the age of seventeen. "Racism led the police of New Jersey to send two innocent men to prison for a combined total of thirty-one years. It was a common attitude in the past and it still persists today," says Jewison.

Norman Jewison was compelled by this story. He explains:

Carter was a man with a great passion for right and justice. Because law-enforcement officials considered him a revolutionary, he was a moving target. I felt that this was a story that needed to be told. I really wanted to tell this story and I did my best to do so with what I felt was an honest interpretation. I feel it was one of my best films.

Jewison based the film on two books, *The 16th Round*, written by Carter himself, and *Lazarus and the Hurricane*, written by Sam Chaiton and Terry Swinton. Jewison then had to work with the screenwriter to narrow the story down. "There were times when we had to eliminate characters because we didn't have the time to develop them. If we had filmed all the scenes in both books, we would have had an eight-hour film," he says.

As it was, the film was three hours long after the first cut. Jewison was willing to make cuts. He explains, "I knew we had to eliminate certain scenes because, as important and as good as they were, the most important thing is the overall structure and rhythm of the whole film. You don't want to lose credibility because if you do, your audience will become bored and you will lose them."

Denzel Washington played the lead. Jewison says:

> To get into the role, Denzel had to lose 40 or 50 pounds [18 to 23 kg] and learn how to box because Carter was a champion boxer. Also Denzel is in his forties and Carter was twenty-nine when he fought for the title. Denzel worked out for a year and a half learning to box, and during the six months before shooting, he practiced two hours every day. I told him, "Denzel, make sure you get a picture of yourself because you'll never look as good again as you do now." The role won him an Academy Award nomination.

One of the things that pleased Jewison was the crew's creative contributions. "Everybody—the actors, the camera operator, the editor, the set designer—all brought their individual talents to the project in ways that I had not foreseen to make the film richer," says Jewison.

Jewison finds that films like *The Hurricane*, in which dramatic stories are combined with social messages, are hard to make in Hollywood today. He believes that the industry has changed dramatically since his first film. "In the past the studios were dominated by a few men who were often considered tyrants by many but who knew the picture business," he explains. "Today, the movie industry is a corporate culture that marketing forces dominate. The subject matter of most films exploits violence for entertainment's sake."

Looking to the Future

While Norman Jewison continues to make films, often with independent companies, he has also played a major role in developing new talent. In 1988, he founded the Canadian Film Centre. Its goal is to train students in the artistic, technical, and business skills of filmmaking. "We wanted to create an institution that would provide the highest-quality learning experience for the best emerging film talent. I believe that in the hands of a skilled artist, the moving image is a sign of change and a custodian of the past," Jewison explains.

In 1999, Norman Jewison was presented with the prestigious Irving G. Thalberg Memorial Award at the Academy Awards in Los Angeles. According to the academy, the award

Norman Jewison holds the Thalberg Award backstage at the Academy Awards ceremony in Los Angeles in 1999.

goes to producers whose work reflects a "consistently high quality." Previous winners include Walt Disney, Alfred Hitchcock, Steven Spielberg, and Clint Eastwood.

Jewison is delighted by the fact that new, low-cost digital equipment has made it possible for many filmmakers to make their own films. He offers this advice to young people today: "Have the courage to follow your dreams. If you have a story you want to tell, pick up a camera—they're cheap enough these days—and make your own film."

Glossary

above-the-line costs—the creative fees paid to producers, writers, directors, and actors
agent—someone who represents another person
animator—a cartoonist who works on paper or with a computer
answer print—the final version of a film
art director—the person who designs and creates the sets
assistant director (AD)—the person who organizes the shooting schedule and coordinates cast and crew
below-the-line costs—crew and staff salaries; equipment, office, and location rental; and legal, insurance, and accounting fees
best boy—an electrician who helps set up the lights; a gaffer's chief assistant
budget—a breakdown of costs
costume designer—the person who designs the actors' costumes
cut—to join together two images of film or videotape in the editing room
dailies—unedited film footage processed directly after shooting for review by the director or producer
digitalization—the conversion of data or graphic images to digital form, usable by a computer
director—the supervisor of the creative efforts of the screenwriters, actors, and crew
director of photography (DP)—the person who supervises the camera crew and designs the lighting and camera movements for each scene. The DP, or cinematographer, does not usually operate the camera on Hollywood features but often does on low-budget films.

distribution—the method used to show a film to an audience. Films are shown in theaters and on television and are also sold or rented. They are shown in other countries too.

documentary—a film about real persons and events. A *cinema verité* film is about an ongoing situation. A historical documentary is about past events.

dolly—a carriage that carries the camera

editing—assembling a motion picture by cutting and rearranging film

executive producer—the person responsible for overall production. The executive producer is involved in hiring talent and reading scripts and may be involved in fund-raising.

feature film—a dramatic movie of a fiction story portrayed by actors whose lines are written in the script. Sometimes called a theatrical or dramatic film, it is shown in theaters and on television.

film—a sheet of celluloid coated with a thin emulsion that records images. The images are invisible until the film is chemically processed in a film laboratory.

fine cut—the next-to-last edited version of a film

gaffer—an electrician who sets up and operates lights

gofer—literally meaning "go for," a person who gets whatever is needed on a film set

grip—a film-crew member who carries equipment, moves sets, places camera accessories, and pushes the dolly for a tracking shot

laboratory—a place in which film is developed and where prints are made

location scout—someone who finds locations for shooting scenes

locations—real places where filming is done, such as a coffee shop or street

mixing session—the blending of sounds and music onto one track

producer—someone who supervises or finances the production of a film or a television program. The producer hires the director—and sometimes the writer and actors—negotiates the deals, works with the writer on the script, raises money, and supervises the schedule and the budget.

production assistant—a person who provides general help, such as controlling street traffic or helping set up equipment

production manager—the person who oversees the daily shooting schedule, the budget, and organizational details of the film or television show

property manager—the person in charge of all the props

props—the items needed in a scene

rough cut—the first edited version of a film, usually without the music tracks and sound effects

scene—a number of shots that present a story or visual idea

script—in a feature film, the script includes the plot, the dialogue, and the visuals of the story

sequence—a series of scenes, usually in the same location, that tell a story

set decorator—the person who arranges the props

shoot—the production process, when the camera records the scene

shot—a single image of a scene. A close-up shows a detail. A medium shot shows the subject waist-high or as part of an environment. A long shot shows the whole person and location. In a dolly shot, the camera is mounted on a four-wheel carriage, called a dolly, and moved during filming. In a tracking shot, the camera moves with the subject at the same speed. Pans move from side to side. Tilts move up and down. Zooms are in-and-out tracking shots.

sound person—the person who records the sound for a film including voice, natural sounds, and music

storyboard—a series of drawings or sketches that outline the major scenes in the story, showing camera angles, locations, costumes, and props

studio—the company that arranges the financing and distribution of a feature film; the place where sets are built

takes—versions of each shot

treatment—a summary or synopsis of the story and idea for a film, television program, or music video

videotape—a magnetic tape on which images and sound are recorded on separate tracks

visual-effects specialist—the person who creates illusionary scenes and persons, often by using a computer

Additional Information

Books

Andersen, Yvonne. *Make Your Own Animated Movies and Videotapes.* Boston: Little, Brown, 1991.

Bone, Jan. *Opportunities in Film Careers.* Lincolnwood, IL: VGM Career Horizons, 1998.

Field, Syd. *Screenplay: The Foundations of Screenwriting.* New York: Dell, 1998.

Hamilton, Jeff. *Special Effects.* New York: Dorling Kindersley, 1998.

Keller, Betty. *Improvisations in Creative Drama: A Program of Workshops and Dramatic Sketches for Students.* Colorado Springs, CO: Meriwether Publishing, 1992.

Kleiler, David, and Robert Moses. *You Stand There: Making Music Video.* New York: Three Rivers Press, 1997.

Linson, Art. *A Pound of Flesh: Perilous Tales of How to Produce Movies in Hollywood.* New York: Grove Press, 1993.

Maltin, Leonard. *Leonard Maltin's Movie Encyclopedia: Career Profiles of More Than 2,000 Actors and Filmmakers, Past and Present.* New York: Viking Press, 1995.

Richards, Andrea. *Girl Director: A How-To Guide for the First-Time, Flat-Broke Film and Video Maker.* Los Angeles: 17th Street Press, 2001.

Singleton, Ralph S. *Filmmaker's Dictionary: Over 5,000 Motion Picture and Television Terms From Technical to Slang.* Los Angeles: Lone Eagle Publishing Company, 2000.

Stevens, Chambers. *Sensational Scenes for Teens: The Scene Studyguide for Teen Actors!* South Pasadena, CA: Sandcastle Publishing, 2001.

Vachon, Christine, and David Edelstein. *Shooting to Kill: How an Independent Producer Blasts Through the Barriers to Make Movies That Matter.* New York: Avon Books, 1998.

Vineyard, Jeremy. *Setting Up Your Shots: Great Camera Moves Every Filmmaker Needs to Know.* Studio City, CA: Michael Wiese Productions, 2000.

Web Sites

Academy of Motion Picture Arts and Sciences
http://www.oscars.org/
For information about past and present winners, the free-admission academy gallery, an events calendar, and the Student Academy Awards for college students

American Film Institute Screen Education Center
http://www.afi.edu/
For a newly launched site with online mini courses on the principles of filmmaking for young people

Canadian Film Centre
http://www.cdnfilmcentre.com/index1.html
For details about special events and film festivals as well as a comprehensive list of links about the film, television, and new media industry

Cyber Film School Moviemaking Web Site
http://www.cyberfilmschool.com/
For monthly columns about producing films, the latest movie reviews, and useful links

Film Festivals.com
http://filmfestivals.com/
For a site that showcases film festivals around the world

International Student Original Film Art Festival
http://www.sofanet.org/
For information about submitting a film to this nonprofit festival started by two high school students to provide young filmmakers the chance to screen their works, receive feedback, and see the work of their peers

Screenwriters Online
www.screenwriter.com
For information about and advice from today's screenwriters

Studentfilms.com
http://studentfilms.com/
For a site with downloadable student films, discussion boards, and useful links

Sundance Online Resource Center
http://www.sundanceonlineresourcecenter.org/
For articles and press releases about the industry and the Sundance Film Festival as well as detailed resource links

Index

Italics indicate illustrations.

Above-the-line costs, 19
The Abyss (feature film), 40
Actors, 58–60, 91, 92
Agents, 34–35
Allen, Woody, 33–34, *33*
And Justice for All (feature film), 92
Art directors, 12
Assistant directors, 11–12

Bamboozled (feature film), 75
Belafonte, Harry, 89
Below-the-line costs, 19
Bernstein, Walter, 26–36, *27*, *33*
  advice for young screenwriters, 36
  childhood, 26–27
  education, 26–27
Best boy, 12
The Black Cat (short film), 51
Black, Stephanie, 76–86, *77*, *79*
  advice for young filmmakers, 86
  childhood, 76
  education, 76, 77, 78
Blacklisting, 29, 30–31, 32, 60
The Blair Witch Project (feature film), 14

Bob Jones University, 55–56
Boys Don't Cry (feature film), 24
Budget, 19–20, 22, 83–84

Camera operators, 11, 63, 67
Canadian Film Centre, 99
Cannes Film Festival, 23, 60
Carrey, Jim, *11*, *41*
Carter, Rubin "Hurricane," 97
The Cincinnati Kid (feature film), 92–94, *93*
Clockers (feature film), 74
Clooney, George, 35, *35*
Costume designers, 12
Curtis, Tony, 90

Dailies, 23
Danger (television series), 31
Detective Story (feature film), 60
Development stage, 9, 19–20
Digitized visual effects, 40–41, 43–44, *45*
Director of photography (DP), 11, 91
Directors, 10–11, 60–64, 89–99
Distribution, 23

Documentaries, 53–57, 61, 62, 68, 79–81, 85–86
Down and Out in America (documentary film), 62
Dramatists Guild, 34
The DuPont Show of the Week (documentary series), 53

Edison, Thomas, 37
Editing, 12, 23, 67–75
The Execution of Mary Stuart (feature film), 38
Eyes on the Prize (documentary TV series), 71

Faces of War (documentary film), 54, *55*
Fail-Safe (feature film), 34, 35
Fail Safe (made-for-TV movie), 35
The Father (feature film), 60–61
Fiddler on the Roof (feature film), 96–97
40 Pounds of Trouble (feature film), 90
4 Little Girls (documentary film), 74–75, *75*
The Front (feature film), 33–34, *33*

Gaffers, 12
Ganja & Hess (feature film), 69
Gofers, 12, 16
Grant, Lee, 58–64, *59, 61, 63*
childhood, 58

education, 59
"green light," 20
grips, 12

H-2 Worker (documentary film), 79–81, *79*
Hampton, Henry, 71
Haynes, Todd, 17
Heller in Pink Tights (feature film), 34
The Hurricane (feature film), 96–99

I Shot Andy Warhol (feature film), 18
In Living Color (television series), *11*
In the Heat of the Night (feature film), 94–96
Industrial Light & Magic (ILM), 39–40

Jacobs, Ken, 76
Jersey, Bill, 48–57, *49, 52, 55*
childhood, 48–49
education, 49
Jewison, Norman, 87–100, *88, 95, 99*
advice for young filmmakers, 100
childhood, 87–88
education, 88
Jungle Fever (feature film), 72

Kanefsky, Victor, 70
Kennedy, Edward, 80
Kennedy, Robert, 94, 96

Kincaid, Jamaica, 86
Kinetoscopes, 38
KRS-One, 81

Lee, Spike, 71, 72, *75*
Lennox, Annie, *82*
Life and Debt (documentary film), 85–86, *85*
Linson, Art, 19
Loyalty and Betrayal (documentary film), 56
Lucas, George, 39, 40

Malcolm X (feature film), 72–73
Manhunt in the Jungle (feature film), 51–53, *52*
The Mask (feature film), 40, *41*
McQueen, Steve, 92–94, *93*
Meisner, Sanford, 59
Méliès, Georges, 39
Miss Evers' Boys (feature film), 35
Mo' Better Blues (feature film), 71, *73*
The Molly Maguires (feature film), 33
Moore, Julianne, 18, *18*
Music videos, 81–85, *82*

The New Yorker (literary magazine), 27
Nobody's Child (feature film), 62–63

Olsen, Tillie, 61, *61*

Pacino, Al, 92
Poison (feature film), 17
Poitier, Sidney, 95
Pollard, Sam, 65–75, *66*, *68*
  childhood, 65–66
  education, 65–67
Postproduction, 12
Preproduction, 9–10, *11*, 91–92
Producers, 10–11, 15–25
Production, 10, *10*, 91
Production assistants, 12
Production managers, 11–12
Profiles
  Bill Jersey, 49
  Christine Vachon, 16
  Habib Zargarpour, 38
  Lee Grant, 59
  Norman Jewison, 88
  Sam Pollard, 66
  Stephanie Black, 77
  Walter Bernstein, 27
Property managers, 12

Rehearsal, 9, 91–92
The Rise and Fall of Jim Crow (documentary TV series), *13*, 56
Ritt, Martin, 33

Safe (feature film), 18
Script breakdown, 20
Script supervisors, 12
Script treatments, 34
Scriptwriting, 28–36, 91
The Season's Change (documentary film), 54

Sesame Street (television series), 86
Set decorators, 12
Set design, 50
Sevigny, Chloë, *24*, 25
Shampoo (feature film), 60
Shot types, 67–68
A Soldier's Story (feature film), 97
Sound person, 11
Special effects. *See* Visual effects.
Star Trek, 40
Star Wars (feature film), 39, 40
Star Wars: Episode I—The Phantom Menace (feature film), 41–46
Steiger, Rod, 95, 96
Story treatments, 19
Sundance Film Festival, 23, 81
Swank, Hilary, 24, *24*, 25
Swoon (feature film), 18

Television scripts, 30
Tell Me a Riddle (feature film), 61
3-2-1 Contact (television series), 70
A Time for Burning (documentary film), 54
Titanic (feature film), 21
Tonight With Belafonte (television series), 89–90

Twister (feature film), 40

Vachon, Christine, 15–25, *16*
childhood, 15–16
education, 16
Van Dyke, Willard, 53
Velvet Goldmine (feature film), 22
Visual effects, 12, *13*, 37–47, *45*
Voyage to the Moon (feature film), 39

Warden, Jack, 92
Washington, Denzel, *73*, 98
Waterworld (feature film), 21
Wayans, Kim, *11*
The Willmar 8 (documentary film), 61
Wyle, Noah, 35, *35*

You Are There (television series), 32
Your Hit Parade (television series), 89

Zargarpour, Habib, *38*, 40–47, *45*
advice for visual-effects students, 46–47
education, 38
childhood, 40

About the Author

Richard Wormser is an accomplished documentary filmmaker and writer who has produced, written, or directed more than 100 films. He is the author of fifteen young adult books for various publishers, including *Defending the Accused: Stories From the Courtroom*, for Franklin Watts. Richard Wormser lives in New York City.

CENTRAL REGIONAL HIGH SCHOOL

36911301013　　　　　791.43 WOR
To the young filmmaker :

CENTRAL REGIONAL HIGH SCHOOL
Media Center
Forest Hills Parkway
Bayville, NJ 08721